Liberating Learning

Liberating Learning

Technology, Politics, and the Future of American Education

Terry M. Moe and John E. Chubb

JOSSEY-BASS
A Wiley Imprint
www.josseybass.com

Published by Jossey-Bass
A Wiley Imprint

989 Market Street, San Francisco, CA 94103-1741—www.josseybass.com

Jossey-Bass books and products are available through most bookstores. To contact Jossey-Bass directly call our Customer Care Department within the U.S. at 800-956-7739, outside the U.S. at 317-572-3986, or fax 317-572-4002.

Jossey-Bass also publishes its books in a variety of electronic formats. Some content that appears in print may not be available in electronic books.

Library of Congress Cataloging-in-Publication Data
Moe, Terry M.
  Liberating learning : technology, politics, and the future of American education / Terry M. Moe and John E. Chubb.—1st ed.
    p. cm.
  Includes bibliographical references and index.
  ISBN 978-0-470-44214-2 (alk. paper)
1. Education—Effect of technological innovations on—United States.   2. Educational technology—Government policy—United States.   3. Public schools—United States.
4. Education and state—United States.   5. Technology and state—United States.   I. Chubb, John E. II. Title.
  LB1028.3.M625 2009
  371.33—dc22
                                                                                    2009004801

Printed in the United States of America
FIRST EDITION
HB Printing 10 9 8 7 6 5 4 3 2

Contents

The Authors

Terry M. Moe is the William Bennett Munro Professor of Political Science at Stanford University, a senior fellow at the Hoover Institution, and a member of the Koret Task Force on K–12 Education. He has also served as a senior fellow at the Brookings Institution in Washington, D.C.

Terry has written extensively on American public education, as well as on the institutions and politics of American government more generally. Along with his many published articles on the nation's education system, he has authored *Schools, Vouchers, and the American Public*, coauthored *Politics, Markets, and America's Schools* with John E. Chubb, and edited *A Primer on America's Schools*.

John E. Chubb is senior executive vice president and chief development officer of EdisonLearning, Inc., which he helped found in 1992. EdisonLearning has partnered with scores of cities and towns to operate or support highly innovative, technologically sophisticated public schools, often serving disadvantaged students. EdisonLearning has recently become a major provider of online education with its acquisition of Provost Systems.

In addition to his work with EdisonLearning, John is a member of the Koret Task Force on K–12 Education and a distinguished visiting fellow at the Hoover Institution at Stanford University. He was previously a senior fellow at the Brookings Institution and a professor of political science at Stanford. His books include *Within Our Reach: How America Can Educate Every Child*; *Bridging the Achievement Gap*, edited with Tom Loveless; and *Politics, Markets, and America's Schools* with Terry M. Moe.

Preface

This is not another pessimistic book about U.S. education. Yes, American students fall short of the standards met by students in many other nations of the world—nations we must compete with economically. Yes, the drop-out rates in our inner city schools are astonishingly high, and there is an alarming gap in achievement between white and minority students. And yes, progress in curing these ills has been slow and unimpressive, even as the need for improvement has accelerated in the twenty-first century. But there is reason for optimism—and the reason is technology.

Yet neither is this another book that just trumpets the wonders of technology. The lives of American young people are being changed every day through the Internet and multipurpose hand-held electronic communications devices (the terms *cell phone* and *computer* barely apply anymore). Information from anywhere in the world, at any time of the day, is available at their fingertips. Schools have access to sophisticated computer programs that use graphics, simulations, and individualized instruction to help students learn in ways the traditional classroom simply cannot. Online technology enables students anywhere—poor inner cities, remote rural areas, even at home—to take any course they like, from the best instructors in the world, and to customize learning to their own needs, schedules, styles, interests, and academic growth. Despite its great promise, however, technology is *not* making American students much smarter or schools much better—at least not yet.

So what is this book, *Liberating Learning*? Above all else, it is a dramatic tale about a struggle for freedom—the freedom of students to learn in the best, most effective ways possible. It is a tale of struggle because technology, owing precisely to its potential for transforming the system, threatens the traditional ways that public education has been carried out in this country for more than a century. It threatens the idea of school as a building, with kids and teachers always concentrated in the same physical place. It threatens the long-standing classroom roles of teachers, generating a variety of new and different jobs and making some of the traditional ones obsolete. It threatens the funding and employment levels of existing schools and districts, as students are provided with exciting new options that allow them to go elsewhere. And much more.

Threats, of course, tend to be resisted in any realm of life. But in public education, we are not talking about any ordinary resistance. Public education is a deeply entrenched government service, and—especially when jobs and money are at issue—it is vigorously protected in the political process by some of the most powerful interest groups in the nation, particularly the teachers unions. For the last quarter century, our nation's leaders have strongly agreed that the public school system is not educating young people as well as it must, and the pressure to improve has been relentless. Yet the results have been disappointing, because the pursuit of truly fundamental reforms—well-enforced accountability for learning, better pay for successful teachers, greater choice of schools for parents, and so forth—have been weakened and often blocked through massive political resistance. Now exactly the same thing is happening with technology. It is being resisted too, and with all the power the defenders can muster.

The question is: what is going to give? Nearly twenty years ago, we wrote about political resistance to change in *Politics, Markets, and America's Schools*. We argued then that the politics of education, driven as it is by the power of special-interest groups, makes it difficult for the nation to embrace reforms that really work

and difficult for schools to adopt any of the well-known practices that enable them to succeed. We went on to argue that, if
possible, public education should be overhauled to give parents
greater choice among schools, to force schools to compete for customers and resources, and to reduce the influence of politics. But
we knew full well that power stood in the way of getting these
reforms in the first place. And we concluded—pessimistically, but
realistically—that unless the politics of public education could be
changed, the schools and the educational prospects of American
kids would not.

Almost twenty years have gone by since we first wrote. During this time, our careers have taken us in different directions.
Terry Moe moved on from the Brookings Institution, where *Politics, Markets, and America's Schools* was researched and written, to
continue a career in academic research at Stanford University and
the Hoover Institution. John Chubb became a founding partner
of the Edison Project, now EdisonLearning, the nation's largest
school management company, which has operated and supported
hundreds of innovative public schools throughout the country.
In very different ways, we have both continued to observe the
struggles of public education, to try to understand them, and to
think about a better future for the nation's schools and children.

Writing together again after many years, and looking out at a
very different world, we now see reason for optimism. The revolution in information technology is historic in its force and scope:
reshaping the fundamentals of how human beings from every
corner of the globe communicate, interact, conduct their business, and simply live their lives from day to day. Education has
so far resisted this revolution, as we could have predicted. But
for reasons we will soon discuss, we believe the resistance will
be overcome—not simply because technology generates innovations of great value for student learning (which it does), but
also, and more fundamentally, because it is destined to have surprising and far-reaching effects on politics and power, and this is
what will ultimately allow the educational changes to go through.

Technology will triumph. But the story of its triumph is a political story.

In writing this book, we have been fortunate to be members of the Koret Task Force on K–12 Education at the Hoover Institution. The task force was created in 1999 by John Raisian, the director of Hoover, with substantial support from the Koret Foundation. He assembled a diverse group of eminent scholars to work together on problems of public education, and to recommend solutions no matter how radical or unorthodox they might need to be. Public education was stagnating. A host of traditional measures were not bringing much improvement. Bolder thinking was needed, and the task force hoped to offer some. The task force included economists Eric Hanushek and Caroline Hoxby; historian Diane Ravitch; literacy authority E. D. Hirsch; psychologist Herbert Walberg; political scientists Bill Evers, Checker Finn, Paul Hill, and Paul Peterson; and the two of us, who are political scientists as well. Recently, E. D. Hirsch retired from the task force, and political scientist Tom Loveless joined.

The Koret Task Force has been a lively forum of intellectual exchange. Our colleagues have challenged our thinking about technology, politics, and education. They have read multiple drafts of this book, and their comments, ideas, and recommendations have surely enhanced the soundness and quality of what we have been able to produce. We owe them a debt of gratitude. We want to thank the Koret Foundation, whose deep concern for better schools and financial support for outside-the-box thinking has made our efforts possible. We also want to express our thanks to John Raisian, whose leadership has kept public education in the forefront of policy research at Hoover and kept the work of the task force very much alive. And finally, we want to thank Sarah Anzia and Jessie Van Rheenen, who served as research assistants on this project and were immensely helpful in bringing our work to fruition.

In conclusion, a brief word about authorship. It is common for coauthors to list their names in alphabetical order, and we followed this convention when we wrote *Politics, Markets and America's Schools*. But inevitably, such an approach may leave the impression that the first author is *the* author, when in fact the work is truly a joint product. For *Liberating Learning*, we are reversing the order of names. But we want to emphasize that both books have been highly collaborative efforts whose ideas and conclusions are the products of our close interaction, working together as a team.

Liberating Learning

1

THE SEEDS OF CHANGE

It doesn't look like a school. It's a small renovated warehouse in Oklahoma City's vibrant "Bricktown" district. The building's third floor can barely hold fifty people. Yet sixty thousand high school students took courses there during the 2006–07 school year. The school is called Advanced Academics, and it provides public education over the Internet to students in twenty-nine states, 140 school districts, and seven "virtual schools" from California to New Jersey and Alaska to Texas. Its students include a range of young people. Some have dropped out of their traditional high schools. Others simply prefer the flexibility of learning at their own pace at home. Still others attend conventional schools, but want Advanced Placement classes that their own schools cannot offer.[1]

The warehouse is home to a top-notch team of technologists, as one might guess. They create the "platform" on which courses are delivered, tests administered and scored, and grades reported to state and local school systems. But mostly the warehouse is home to teachers—about thirty in all. For the education offered here is not strictly digital. Every course is supported by a teacher who is fully certified and even "highly qualified" under the federal government's No Child Left Behind accountability regulations.[2]

The teachers instruct their students as they work through digital lessons or complete assignments. Some of the instruction comes through written "instant messages"; some occurs via whiteboard correspondence, with both teacher and student sketching ideas on the same electronic surface; some involves Internet phone calls. Teachers also provide detailed comments on student essays and research papers, including electronic edits and suggestions for revisions. Because teachers are doing less direct instruction than in a traditional classroom, they have more time to respond to student questions and work. They typically support four or five students at a time from their computers, providing a level of individual attention they could never offer to a regular high school class. All of the teachers here have taught in traditional public schools, but see advantages for students in the differentiation afforded by online instruction.

Teachers like the informal, collegial atmosphere of the warehouse, where they easily interact all day long, sharing student challenges, and brainstorming strategies. They enjoy the flexible hours. The warehouse is buzzing with teaching from 7:00 AM to 11:00 PM. They can choose from a variety of hours, as students take their online courses around the clock, day and night. Some teachers work mornings and evenings so they can be at home with their young children in the afternoons. They are also given one day a week to work from home—but only one day, for the give-and-take of the warehouse helps teachers develop their online skills together.

School need not mean one teacher and twenty-five students in a series of classrooms. The little warehouse in Oklahoma City is one of many places around the country now offering instruction to students who are located long distances from the "school." In 2006, the most recent year with authoritative data, nearly three-quarters of a million public school students completed courses online.[3]

Electronic instruction is changing conventional schoolhouses as well. In Dayton, Ohio, for example, students in two schools, Dayton Academy and Dayton View Academy, both K–8 charter schools, returned from summer vacation in 2007 to find their schools physically transformed.[4] Large state-of-the-art learning labs and media centers replaced traditional libraries and cramped computer labs. In their regular classrooms students found minia-ture laptops, packaged in kid-friendly hard plastic. On the laptops were "task managers" that showed each student the cus-tomized assignments to be carried out in the new instructional spaces. Teachers also had powerful new management tools. In the lab, they could view every student's computer on a touch screen—revealing how quickly students were progressing through a lesson, whether they had a question, whether they were mak-ing too many mistakes. Teachers had new electronic assignment books and gradebooks to keep track of what their students were accomplishing electronically as well as traditionally.

In the Dayton Academies, students are spending forty-five minutes per day in grades K–5 and ninety minutes per day in grades 6–8 in the learning lab or media center. In both set-tings their instruction is in double-size classes of about sixty students, supported by a *single* classroom teacher—and, in the media center, by a library media specialist as well. The higher student-teacher ratios during the electronically supported instruc-tional periods have enabled the schools to reduce the number of teachers they normally required. The staff savings have been used to raise the compensation of teachers and administrators, which in turn has enabled the schools to attract and retain stronger educators.

Dayton is a highly competitive charter school market. Half of all the sixty public schools are now charters, including twelve of the top twenty academic performers in the district.[5] And because the Dayton Academies are schools of choice, with no guaranteed clientele, they need to perform at high levels in order to keep their students, families, and revenues. As charter schools, they have the freedom to do that in novel ways—and they have embraced technology with a passion, showing that even brick-and-mortar schools that look wholly conventional on the outside can be trans-formed on the inside. Teachers and students still gather together in buildings, face-to-face. But teaching is different. And learning is different.

America's Schools

These schools are exciting in their own right. What they are doing is innovative, and a striking departure from the traditional ways that American schools have long done their business. But they are also exciting because of what they represent. They are part of a movement, now in its early stages, to bring the revolution in information technology to public education, and in so doing, to harness its enormous potential for transforming—and improving—the way children learn, the way teachers teach, and the way schools are organized and operated.

What technology offers is profoundly important to the nation. America desperately needs to improve its public schools, and virtually everyone in a position of knowledge or public responsibility agrees that this is the case. The broad consensus among our policymakers—Democrat and Republican, liberal and conservative, from all corners of the country—is that the public schools are not delivering the goods, and that something serious needs to be done to turn the situation around.

This consensus is not new. It emerged in the wake of the most influential report ever issued on the quality of American education, A Nation at Risk, which argued in 1983 that the United States was facing "a rising tide of mediocrity" in its schools.[6] The response at the time was remarkable: a frenzied push for reform that, within just a few years, left no state untouched. Even more remarkable, this frenzy has continued unabated ever since, to the point that education reform has become the new status quo. It is what the nation does, year after year, as a matter of routine. All this activity, however, has not led to a significant boost in school performance. The fact is, the reform process has never ended because the reforms have typically led to disappointment—and to demands for still more reforms. So here the nation is, after a quarter century of perpetual effort and huge expense, and the state of public education remains troubling.

To be sure, there is still much to be proud of. America's public schools are a venerable democratic tradition. This country was the first in the world to value a free education for every child, regardless of economic circumstance or social status, and throughout the 1800s and most of the 1900s, it took major strides in getting children enrolled, keeping them enrolled through high school, socializing immigrant populations, promoting democratic principles, and sending growing numbers of students to college. It was the envy of the world, and deservedly so.[7]

Over the last half century, however, the schools have faced new and daunting challenges, driven in large measure by globalization, intense international competition, and a heightened emphasis on education— which scholars have shown to be a critical determinant of a nation's productivity and growth. In the modern world, economic prosperity cannot be secured through high school diplomas and basic skills, the nation's recipe for most of the twentieth century. It takes much more than that: analytic thinking, problem solving, independence, the ability to seek out and assimilate new knowledge.[8]

The public schools have not met this modern challenge—and the nation is still at risk. They have made some progress over the last few decades, especially among minorities, and that deserves to be recognized. But "some" progress is not nearly enough. Even today, regardless of the subject matter, the vast majority of America's students are not proficient by national standards. And test scores of minorities remain far below those of whites, producing a glaring achievement gap the schools have been unable to close. Meanwhile, American students continue to do unimpressively in tests of international achievement—and the older the students, the farther they fall behind their counterparts in many other developed countries.[9]

For the nation as well as for individual students, these gaps in educational performance matter more and more every day. The world is becoming more competitive, not less. The industries and jobs that promise prosperity in the future are increasingly dependent on higher levels of education. Nations such as India and China, which as recently as a decade ago were hardly factors in international competition, now compete aggressively and powerfully in economic markets, and their economies are growing at astronomical rates. Thomas Friedman recently detailed a world with a radically decentralized and newly leveled economic playing field—a world that, transformed by technological change, had essentially become "flat."[10] America's ability to prosper in such a world, he argued, critically depends on its ability to educate its citizens more effectively.

No one disagrees with this assessment: the increasing value of education is recognized by one and all, regardless of ideology or party allegiance. But will America's schools ever take the leap forward that a bright future so clearly demands? And will technology help it do that?

The Benefits of Technology

The schools we described above, one in Oklahoma and two in Ohio, are unknown to most Americans. And as innovations, they barely make a ripple in the vast sea that is the nation's public school system. But they are harbingers of things to come.

Like so many other novelties that surround us these days, from iPods to YouTube to Wikipedia, they are expressions of a profound social force—the revolution in information technology—that while still in process, is fast generating one of the most important transformations in all of human history. Because we are all enmeshed in this revolution every day, most of us are naturally inclined to take it for granted as a normal part of our lives, and to have a difficult time appreciating the enormity of its longer-term implications. But the fact is, it is radically changing our world.

The information revolution has globalized the international economy, made communication and social networking—among anyone, anywhere—virtually instantaneous and costless, put vast storehouses of information and research within reach of everyone on the planet, dramatically boosted the prospects of cooperation and collective action, internationalized the cultures of previously insulated nations, and in countless other ways transformed the fundamentals of human society. The new schools in Oklahoma and Ohio are an integral part of all this. They are among the first stirrings of a revolution in how children can learn and be educated.

The possibilities are exciting—and astounding. Even today, with educational technology in its earliest stages:

- Curricula can be customized to meet the learning styles and life situations of individual students, giving them productive alternatives to the boring standardization of traditional schooling.

- Education can be freed from geographic constraint: students and teachers do not have to meet in a building within a school within a district, but can be anywhere, doing their work at any time.

- Students can have more interaction with their teachers and with one another, including teachers and students who may be thousands of miles away or from different nations or cultures.

- Parents can readily be included in the communications loop and involved more actively in the education of their kids.

- Teachers can be freed from their tradition-bound classroom roles, employed in more differentiated and productive ways, and offered new career paths.

- Sophisticated data systems can put the spotlight on performance, make progress (or the lack of it) transparent to all concerned, and sharpen accountability.

- Schools can be operated at lower cost, relying more on technology (which is relatively cheap) and less on labor (which is relatively expensive).

These advantages only begin to describe the educational promise of technology, and it is guaranteed to continue generating innovations at a breathtaking pace in the years ahead. The great power of technology is that no one really knows what it will produce or make possible in the future. Who would have thought, not so long ago, that such a thing as the Internet could even exist? Or that any child could use a laptop computer to gain access to massive compendiums of information on virtually any topic of interest? These are mind-blowing developments.

Although the advance of educational technology is still in its early stages, there can be little doubt that the information revolution has the capacity to revolutionize education. It could hardly be otherwise. Information and knowledge are absolutely fundamental to what education is all about—to what it means, in fact, for people to become educated—and it would be impossible for the information revolution to unfold and *not* have transformative implications for how children can be educated and how schools and teachers can more productively do their jobs.

But to say that technology is hugely beneficial and that it has the capacity to revolutionize American education does not mean that this revolution is actually going to happen.[11] That is the question at hand, the question this book is written to address. Will the promise of technology be realized in practice—and transform and improve the nation's public schools?

Political Resistance

The answer might seem obvious. Given the stagnation in performance that has long plagued American education, and given the long-standing inability of reform efforts to bring real improvement, the revolution in information technology clearly opens up exciting opportunities for revitalizing the education system and making it much more productive. Surely these opportunities will be greeted with open arms and put to creative use in promoting innovation, driving change, and doing what is best for kids. Surely technology will triumph—and transform the education system.

But this line of argument is too easy. It focuses on the force for change—the benefits of technology—and there is much more to the story than that. Consider the plight of the Wisconsin Virtual Academy (WVA), a charter school operated by Wisconsin's Northern Ozaukee school district in cooperation with K12 Inc., a for-profit company. This school is one of the pioneers in bringing distance-learning technologies to public education: providing a rigorous, customized curriculum to students who "attend" from locations all over the state of Wisconsin, and whose needs were not being met by their own districts. Exciting, right? But also threatening to the districts that are losing students and resources to this innovative school. And threatening to the state teachers union, which, among other things, wants to protect the jobs of teachers in those districts, and does not like WVA's ability (facilitated by technology) to operate at lower teacher-student ratios. So the teachers union went to court to have WVA—and implicitly, all schools like it in the state of Wisconsin—put out of business, claiming that the school's mode of operation violates existing state education laws (which were written without distance learning in mind).

We'll continue this story in a later chapter. But what it represents is something quite fundamental. The force of technology is up against a counterforce: resistance by groups that do not want the traditional education system to change. Precisely because technology promises to transform the core components of schooling, it is inevitably disruptive to the jobs, routines, and resources of the people whose livelihoods derive from the existing system—and these people are represented by organizations that are extraordinarily powerful in politics. They are trying to use that power to prevent technology from transforming American education. And they will continue to do so in the future.

This mobilization of power to block change is not unique to technology. It is, in microcosm, the saga of American education reform. America has been dissatisfied with the performance of its public schools for decades now, and has persistently tried to reform and improve them, but with disappointing results. A prime reason for all the disappointment is that reforms that really promise to change things are also threatening to groups with material stakes in the existing system—and throughout the reformist era, they have used their political power to prevent major change and preserve the status quo. This being so, the American education system faces much more than a performance problem. It also faces a *political* problem that, in the grander scheme of things, is more fundamental than the performance problem itself—because it prevents the performance problem from being seriously addressed and resolved.

The political problem that hamstrings American education is in fact a common problem throughout American government, and deeply rooted in the nature of things. For there are vested interests—groups with a material stake in the status quo—in *every* area of public policy, and they tend to be organized, powerful, and quite successful at using the political process to prevent reform within their own policy domains. Why is it so difficult for the United States to move toward a more rational and comprehensive health care system, and thus to resolve what most experts regard as a very serious performance problem? A prime reason is that insurance companies, pharmaceutical companies, and other businesses with a vested interest in the current health care system are threatened by any major overhaul, and they use their considerable power in the political process to block. Why does the nation continue to subsidize cotton, soybeans, and other crops—including tobacco, one of the most harmful substances in American society—when most experts agree that the subsidies make no good sense and the system should be radically changed? Here too, the main reason this problem can't be resolved is that farmers, tobacco companies, and related businesses with a vested interest in the system are politically powerful, and they use their power to block any shift to a new policy.

To say that the deck is stacked against change in public education, then, is simply to recognize a basic reality of government and politics. A stacked deck is normal. And so is the expectation that, as technology generates new ideas and possibilities with great promise for American education, political power will be wielded to put a lid on what technology can really do—and to ensure that the revolution in information technology does *not* transform the traditional education system.

The Future

The nation's schools will only be transformed if this political resistance can somehow be overcome. This is a tall order, to say the least, for it reflects the very same political problem that education reforms of all types have been up against—and largely defeated by—for decades. Why should technology be any different? When all is said and done, this is the pivotal issue.

The central claim of our book is that technology *is* different. It is different, of course, because of its sheer enormity as a historic social force, and because of the great benefits it promises for learning and education. But these drivers of change are not enough to overcome the inevitable resistance. What sets technology apart from other sources of reform is that, as we will discuss in our final chapter, it also has a far-reaching capacity to *change politics*—and to eat away, relentlessly and effectively, at the political barriers that have long prevented reform. Technology, then, is a double-barreled agent of change. It generates the innovations that make change attractive, and at the same time it undermines the political resistance that would normally prevent change from happening. It pushes for change—and opens the political gates.

This is not to say that the triumph of technology will come easily, because it won't. There will be struggles and setbacks, and the process will take decades. But the forces of resistance will ultimately be overcome, leading to a transformation of the American school system. This will mean real improvement, and real benefits for the nation and its children. It will also mean something still more profound: the dawning of a new era in which politics is more open, productive ideas are more likely to flourish—and learning is liberated from the dead hand of the past.

2

THE NEED FOR ACHIEVEMENT

Technology is coming to education, and that's a very good thing. It's good because it allows for the customization of learning, for more effective teaching, for a vast expansion in the courses and learning opportunities available to students, and for all sorts of other possibilities. But it's also good because this is a time of great need. The nation has a performance problem: a weakness in its educational system that policymakers have been unable to overcome despite decades of continuous effort and gargantuan expense. The levels of student achievement that prevail in modern America are unacceptably low—and this magnifies the value of what technology has to contribute.

To appreciate what technology has to offer, then, and why it stands to have such a big and positive impact, we need to begin with a clear picture of the current state of affairs. How well are America's students really performing? How much have they improved over the years? How do they stack up to kids in other nations?

A Long Way from Proficiency

See how your knowledge of science stacks up against the nation's young people.

A human CANNOT survive the loss of which of the following?
A) Appendix
B) Liver

C) Lung
D) Kidney

If you answered "Liver," you are doing better than nearly 60 percent of the nation's eighth-grade students. On the 2005 National Assessment of Education Progress (or NAEP) science test, only 42 percent of eighth graders knew that human beings can survive without an appendix, without a lung, or without a kidney—but not without a liver.[1] On another test item, only 17 percent knew that the earth's atmosphere is made up mostly of nitrogen and oxygen—a percentage worse than random guessing would yield on a four-option multiple-choice question.[2] On another, a full 60 percent thought that condensation was the same as melting, evaporating, or even sweating.[3]

The NAEP tests have been administered regularly since 1969 to a representative cross section of American students, and provide what is often referred to as the "nation's report card." They are rigorously designed to capture what students ought to be learning across a range of basic subjects, and they are the closest thing the nation has to a gold standard for measuring levels of student achievement as well as changes and trends over time.[4]

It is widely accepted—and for good reason—that student achievement in the United States is disappointing. But what does "disappointing" mean, more concretely? To put some meat on the bones, let's take a broad summary look at what the NAEP test results have to say, focusing on the percentage of students who score "proficient" on the various exams—a score high enough to show that they have acquired the knowledge and skills that NAEP's experts believe are appropriate for the relevant grade level.[5]

Consider, for instance, how the nation's eighth graders recently performed in science, an area of knowledge that could hardly be more important to America's future in a globalized, technology-driven economy. In 2005, just 27 percent of them earned a score of proficient or better. By the standards of NAEP, then, nearly three-quarters don't know what they ought to know for their grade level. Indeed, of this huge group of nonproficient students, more than half have learned so little that their performance is labeled "below basic"—which is *far* below grade level and clearly troubling.

Science is hardly the only problem area. Test results are similarly distressing for every subject. On the most recent U.S. history test, given in 2006, only 17 percent of all eighth graders were proficient or better.[6] On the civics exam, given the same year, only 22 percent of eighth graders were proficient or better.[7] And on the 2007 test of reading, the most important of all academic skills, only 31 percent of eighth graders scored proficient or better.[8] Remarkably, 26 percent of all eighth-grade students tested below basic in reading, a skill level equivalent to functional illiteracy.[9]

Perhaps our young people are better at math. Consider another recent test question.

The sum of three numbers is 173. If the smallest number is 23, could the largest number be 62?
Yes
No

Math, like science, is a skill of increasing value in the modern economy, and it is vital to technological innovation, where jobs of the future will increasingly lie. Math is also taught daily to students from kindergarten forward—more regularly by far than science, which is not one of the proverbial "3 R's"—so one would expect higher achievement for math than science. But this is barely the case. On the NAEP 2007 math test, only 31 percent of American eighth graders scored proficient or better.[10] No surprise, then, that even a math question as simple as the above "sum of three numbers" item stumped most of them. If three numbers sum to 173, and two of them are 23 and 62, then the third would have to be 88. Which is obviously larger than 62. So the answer to the question—requiring nothing more than rudimentary addition and subtraction—is "No." But only 42 percent of eighth graders managed to get it right.[11] (Half of them should have gotten it right by guessing randomly.)

These recent test results for eighth graders help to illustrate the current state of affairs in American education: our children are not performing at levels that equip them, or the nation, for the rigors of the twenty-first century. To get a sense of the bigger picture, let's turn to Table 2.1, which provides NAEP data on more academic subjects, students of different ages and ethnicities, and changes over time.[12]

The early data we present here begin in 1990 or shortly thereafter. The actual base years are slightly different for different academic subjects, depending on the specific years in which they were tested. We chose the early 1990s because it is far enough in the past to allow for significant improvement, but recent enough to have tests that use the same frameworks in use today to measure what students know. It is worth adding that 1990 roughly marks the point at which both the school accountability and the school choice movements began to surge, which means that we will be looking at test score changes over an especially intense period of school reform.[13]

Consider the scores for reading, the most fundamental of academic skills. Among American fourth graders as a whole, 27 percent were reading proficiently in 1992, and 32 percent were reading proficiently in 2007, for a small gain of 5 percent—a gain that still leaves the *level* of proficiency quite low. To get a more refined sense of how proficiency has changed over time, however, we need to recognize that the ethnic composition of the student population has changed during this period. In particular, Hispanic students—many of whom do not speak English as a first language, and may just be learning it—made up 7 percent of the test takers in 1992, but were 17 percent of the test takers in 2007. It is more revealing, then, to break down the national test scores by ethnic group to get a clearer sense of what is going on.

Table 2.1 National Assessment of Education Progress

Percentages of Students Proficient or Advanced 1990–1996 compared to 2005–2007

Subject/Grade	All		White		Black		Hispanic	
	1990s	2000s	1990s	2000s	1990s	2000s	1990s	2000s
Reading (4th)	27	32	33	42	8	14	12	17
Reading (8th)	27	29	33	38	8	12	11	14
Reading (12th)	37	34	44	41	16	15	20	18
Math (4th)	12	39	15	51	1	15	4	22
Math (8th)	15	31	18	41	5	11	7	15
Math (12th)	NC	22	NC	28	NC	5	NC	7
Science (4th)	26	27	34	38	5	5	8	10
Science (8th)	27	27	35	38	4	7	10	10
Science (12th)	21	17	27	23	3	2	6	5
History (4th)	16	17	20	25	4	5	3	5
History (8th)	12	15	15	22	2	3	3	5
History (12th)	10	12	12	16	2	2	3	4

The data have been collected from the NAEP Data Explorer data tool on the NAEP Web site. Go to http://nces.ed.gov/nationsreportcard/naepdata/. For the various subjects, the specific beginning and ending test years in the table are: Reading 4th and 8th (1992–2007), Reading 12th (1992–2005), Math 4th and 8th (1990–2007), Math 12th (2005—earlier tests are not comparable, NC), Science (1996–2005), and United States History (1994–2006).

When this is done, we see that all three of the ethnic groups depicted here actually made somewhat bigger gains than the national averages would suggest: 9 percent for whites, 6 percent for blacks, and 5 percent for Hispanics. Yet even these larger gains are hardly large in any meaningful sense, because the levels of proficiency remain low. White fourth graders do best, at 42 percent proficient—but this means that most of them still do not know what NAEP believes they ought to know for their grade level. And the figures are dramatically worse—14 percent proficient and 17 percent proficient, respectively—for black and Hispanic fourth graders. These numbers are disturbingly low, and a clear indication that something is very wrong. Yes, there has been progress, but the progress is a drop in the bucket compared to where the nation—and these children—need to be. The achievement gap that divides the races, moreover, has actually widened during this period of time: a period of intense reform in which considerable effort and money were invested in closing that gap.

At the higher grades, the story of reading achievement gets worse. By comparison to fourth graders, eighth graders made gains from 1992 to 2007 that are uniformly smaller for all ethnic groups; and for each ethnic group, the 2007 proficiency outcomes are in the same low range. The twelfth graders, moreover, gain even less than the eighth graders. Indeed, the twelfth graders—who have been in the American K–12 education system the longest and best reflect what it has to offer—actually declined across this period: 3 percent fewer whites were proficient, 1 percent fewer blacks, and 2 percent fewer Hispanics. The achievement gap separating whites from blacks and Hispanics, meanwhile, is just as much in evidence among these older kids as it is among the fourth graders. And here too, the gap is not closing over time.

Math is a brighter picture. From 1990 to 2007, the percentage of students scoring proficient rose considerably in grades four and eight. Among white fourth graders, those demonstrating proficiency jumped from 15 percent to 51 percent; among blacks, from 1 to 15 percent; and among Hispanics, from 4 to 22 percent. For eighth graders, the gains were in the same range, but somewhat smaller in magnitude. Progress for twelfth graders could not be evaluated over this period, because their test was reformulated, and the later scores are not comparable to the earlier ones. Based on the available evidence, though, the overall picture for math is one of progress.

But this progress needs to be understood in context. Math performance began the period with proficiency levels roughly half those of reading, which were themselves quite low. Even with substantial gains, most of the nation's students were still not proficient in math by 2007—and among minorities, the percentage not proficient remained astronomical. The achievement gap has widened, and the evidence suggests that math gains may be especially difficult to make with the neediest populations. The evidence also suggests that math gains become tougher as students move up in grade levels and the skills expected of them become more sophisticated. On the new NAEP grade twelve math test, administered in 2005, fully 72 percent of all white twelfth graders were not proficient in math, and the figure climbed to 95 percent for blacks and 93 percent for Hispanics. We do not know precisely how these outcomes compare to those of earlier years, when the test was significantly different. But we do know that substantially fewer students are achieving high standards at twelfth grade than at eighth and fourth: an ominous sign as students move on to higher education or into the workforce.

And math is the standout. The picture in science and U.S. history is even worse than in reading. Although science is clearly of key importance to children as they—and the nation—move into an increasingly high-tech future, science scores have improved only slightly (a few points) over the last fifteen years for fourth and eighth graders, and the level of proficiency in 2005 remains low. In both grades, almost two-thirds of white students are not proficient, and among minorities it is roughly 90 percent. High school seniors are worse still; their percentage scoring proficient actually declined over the last fifteen years, and the levels of nonproficiency are huge: 77 percent for whites, 98 percent for blacks, and 95 percent for Hispanics.

The results for U.S. history are no better. All age groups have made slight progress, but achievement remains low. Among white fourth and eighth graders, roughly three-fourths fail to reach proficiency, and among blacks and Hispanics about 95 percent miss the mark. For twelfth graders, once again, the scores are even worse: 84 percent of the white students are not proficient, along with 98 percent of the black students and 96 percent of the Hispanic students. History is a subject that teaches facts—which are surely an indispensable part of knowledge—but it also offers a grander perspective on societies and their institutions, an appreciation of context and culture, skills of social analysis, and other important foundations for living a productive life and becoming a good citizen. Most of what the teaching of history has to offer, however, appears to be lost on America's students. They are not benefiting much. And neither is the nation.

NAEP scores provide the best evidence available on the academic achievement of U.S. children, and the summary judgment is not good: the level of achievement is too low, and progress (except in math) has been sluggish and inadequate. In rounding out the picture, we should also point out that children can't learn—and aren't included in the testing—if they drop out of the education process. Traditionally, Americans have justly been proud of the nation's long-standing dedication to getting all children into school and keeping them there until graduation. But the fact is that the percentage of kids graduating from high school is much lower than government statistics have suggested over the years, in part because the figures are difficult to calculate. In recent years, scholars have developed new methods, and the evidence is eye-opening. For the nation as a whole, the high school on-time graduation rate for 2003 was only 70 percent.[14] The on-time graduation rate for 1991 was 72 percent.[15] Both rates are unacceptably low, and quite out of keeping with the goal of seeing that all kids get educated. Despite all the reform efforts during the 1990s, moreover, there has clearly been *no progress:* the graduation rate has actually declined a bit.

These graduation figures are important for what they tell us about the nation as a whole. We also need to recognize, however, that the kids who are at greatest risk are low-income minorities, who tend to be clustered in large urban school districts—and for these kids, graduation rates are much lower than the national average. In Milwaukee, for example, only 39 percent of African American students graduated from high school on time. In Cleveland, it was 47 percent. In Detroit, 43 percent. The graduation rates for Hispanic students are comparable (although they tend to be concentrated in different districts): 44 percent in Los Angeles, 33 percent in New York City, 41 percent in Denver.[16] The American education system is letting these kids down. For the kids who stay in school, there is an achievement gap of sizable proportions that hasn't gone away with time and reform. And on top of that, enormous numbers of these kids do not stay in school long enough to graduate—and are entirely unprepared to play productive roles in a competitive economy.

Lagging the World

As the modern world grows smaller, flatter, and more competitive, the achievement of American students must be measured not only against national standards, but also against international ones. Work and jobs quickly shift around the globe to whoever can perform them at the highest quality and the lowest price. Distance, language, and politics—factors that once limited international economic integration—have diminished greatly in importance, and the Internet has enabled the instantaneous sharing and internationalization of work. It is now common in manufacturing, for example, for products to be assembled of components that have been produced in multiple nations around the world. Nations that once did not consume what was produced in the West, or produce anything the West would consume—nations such as China, India, and the former Soviet Union, as well as countries throughout Eastern Europe and much of the Middle East—now participate fully in a much larger and dynamic world economy than existed just a generation ago.

These developments stand to enrich our children's lives culturally, socially, intellectually, and aesthetically, as more and different people share with one another their ideas, traditions, and accomplishments. These developments also have the potential to improve the living standards of the next generation of Americans. A larger world economy means more markets for the goods and services Americans produce. It means a larger economic pie for everyone to divide. But the slice America's young people will receive depends heavily on the knowledge and skills they bring to the global marketplace. The greatest economic returns will go to the best educated, to those who can keep pace with rapid technological change, to those who can create the industries that have not even been thought of today.[17]

The jobs that once supported the American middle class required only a high school education. These jobs began moving overseas twenty to thirty years ago, and they will continue to do so. Over the last seventy-five years the United States doubled the percentage of adults that completed high school and tripled the percentage that earned a college degree. This progress helped fuel the rise of domestic living standards—but it is not nearly enough to meet the challenges of the more competitive, technologically driven world the nation is now faced with. Education is more crucial than ever, and a "basic" education no longer cuts it. The issue, increasingly, is how well America's children—and therefore its future workers—compare to their counterparts in other nations around the globe.[18]

On this front, the news is hardly uplifting. The most recent data, from the Program for International Assessment (PISA) in 2006, measures the achievement of fifteen-year-old students in 30 Organisation for Economic Co-operation and Development (OECD) nations (which, like the United States, are among the more economically advanced) and 28 non-OECD nations (which tend to be poorer). The most meaningful comparisons, of course, are between the United States and other OECD nations, and what they reveal is unsettling: U.S. students ranked 21st out of 30 OECD nations in science, and 25th out of 30 in math—well below the international average of advanced nations.[19] Their achievement was most comparable to students in Iceland, the Slovak Republic, Spain, and Portugal. These results are consistent with the 2003 PISA exam, which showed that the United States ranked 18th out of 28 OECD nations in science and 23rd out of 28 in math.[20]

The low scores are not due to a more democratic mix of students in the United States. The fact is, America's very best students are not competitive either. Compared to students at the 95th percentile of their respective test score distributions, America's top students ranked 13th out of 30 OECD nations on the PISA 2006 science test. If the focus is instead on American students with economic advantages—those from families high in socioeconomic status (SES)—performance is even more mediocre: these advantaged American students ranked 18th out of 30 compared to high SES students internationally.

On the other side of the ledger, one might still hope that America's most disadvantaged students would not rank among the lowest in the world. The United States, after all, has historically been a leader in extending free public education to every child regardless of circumstance. Unfortunately, PISA 2006 shows that America's low SES students rank 24th in science relative to low SES students in 30 OECD nations. It also points up one statistic on which the United States *is* among the world "leaders": the difference in achievement between high and low SES students. The achievement gap in the United States is the 4th largest of the 30 OECD nations studied.[21] Although lamentable, this is not so surprising given what we know about NAEP scores and their enormous and persistent differences across ethnic groups.

While PISA studies fifteen-year-olds, other programs have carried out international comparisons of younger students. The best-known of these is the Trends in International Math and Science Study (TIMMS), whose most recent results are for 2007.[22] As we might expect, having seen the patterns in domestic NAEP scores, America's younger kids generally seem to do better against international competition than the older kids do. The rankings are less clear than they might appear, however, because the countries included in these studies are quite different. The PISA studies are actually carried out under the aegis of OECD itself, so all 30 OECD countries participate. But TIMMS is carried out by another organization (the International Association for the Evaluation of Education Achievement, known as the IEA), and in 2007 many of the OECD countries did not participate. Just 11 of them took part in the eighth-grade exam, and 15 in the fourth-grade exam. Many of the countries that chose not to participate in 2007—for example, Korea (for fourth grade), Finland, Canada, and Switzerland—are countries that, judging by other exam outcomes, may well have scored ahead of the United States on TIMMS had they taken the test.

The ray of sunshine in the TIMMS 2007 exam is that the nation's fourth graders are doing pretty well by international standards. On the fourth-grade science exam, the United States ranked 3rd out of the 15 OECD countries that participated—a very decent performance. Yet on the eighth-grade science exam, the United States didn't do as well, ranking 6th out of 11 OECD countries, right in the middle of the pack. And more important, these rankings are not the same as ranking 3rd or 6th out of the full set of 30 OECD countries, because some of the nonparticipating countries probably would have outscored the United States had they taken the test. Indeed, if we simply include in these comparisons four economically developed countries that took the test but are not members of OECD—Singapore, Taiwan, Hong Kong, and Russia—the bloom comes off the rose by a good bit. With this adjustment, the U.S. ranking for fourth-grade science is 7th out of 19 advanced nations, and its ranking for eighth-grade science is 10th out of 15.

The TIMMS math results for 2007 are comparable. On the fourth-grade exam, the United States ranked 4th out of the 15 participating OECD countries; but if Singapore, Taiwan, Hong Kong, and Russia are included, the United States ranking drops to 8th out of 19. The eighth graders, as we've come to expect, do somewhat worse. At this level, the United States ranked 5th out of the 11 participating OECD nations, and 9th out of 15 when the other four advanced nations are included in the comparisons. If the United States hopes to maintain its leadership role in the world economy during the coming century, these sorts of middling outcomes in math—and in science as well—do not bode well. They are not bad. They are just not the foundation on which true economic leadership can be sustained.

The PISA 2006 and TIMMS 2007 exams are but two of many international tests that have been administered over the years. Recent research by Stanford economist Eric Hanushek and associates has "normalized" the various international exams to a common scale so that they can more readily be aggregated to yield a composite picture of international performance over time. Their analysis shows that, beginning in the 1960s and 1970s, the United States ranked poorly compared to other economically advanced nations—and that, although the United States has improved its test scores over the years, so have most other advanced nations. The United States continues to rank well down in the pack. Its aggregated scores during the 2000s put it at 17th in a group of 25 OECD countries in the study.[23]

Education and the International Economy

Economic research also shows that it matters enormously how well nations do on achievement tests, and thus it matters that the United States does so poorly. It matters because the test scores—as measures of a nation's underlying level of cognitive skills—turn out to have a huge impact on economic growth, even when a full range of other factors are statistically controlled. By Hanushek's estimates, if the United States had been able to increase its educational performance from its middling levels in past decades to the level of the international educational leaders by year 2000, its gross domestic product would by 2015 be 4.5 percent higher than it would otherwise have been. This is a staggering difference, and translates into an increase in national income equal to the entire amount (approximately $500 billion annually) that the United States currently spends on its entire K–12 education system.[24]

Cognitive skills are a good indicator of a nation's "human capital." Another is the number of years of schooling that its citizens receive—their levels of educational "attainment"—which has also been shown through research to be a determinant of economic growth. Historically, the United States led the world in attainment levels. It built an education system open to all, and was highly successful (compared to other nations) at getting its children into school and keeping them there. But while many Americans may think that this is still true, it isn't. Other nations have now overtaken us, to the point that the United States is now *below the OECD average* in educational attainment.[25] Thus, just as the data on cognitive skills reflect poorly on the relative quality of education in the United States, so the data on attainment reflect poorly on its quantity.

But what about once the K–12 years of education are over? One often hears that U.S. students catch up with the world in college. American universities have long been and continue to be the envy of the world. Millions of students from around the globe attend universities in the United States, and the number increases annually. Even so, the presence of this asset has not provided unambiguous advantages to American students. About 30 percent of American adults hold a bachelor's degree or higher, which is a middling percentage compared to other industrialized nations.

More striking differences emerge if we look at advanced degrees, and in particular at concentrations in science and engineering—subjects in great demand for the twenty-first century economy. In 2005, 13.7 percent of the advanced degrees (generally master's and doctorate) earned by U.S. students were in science and 6.4 percent in engineering. Of the advanced degrees earned by Japanese students, by contrast, 38.5 percent were in science and 38.5 percent in engineering.[26] That's four times as frequent a focus on technical degrees in Japan as in the United States. In Korea, science commanded 45.6 percent of advanced degrees and engineering 32.3 percent. Even the United Kingdom, culturally similar to the United States, had higher percentages: 21.0 percent science and 8.4 percent engineering. Among 26 OECD nations surveyed, American students ranked 23rd in science and 16th in engineering as percentages of advanced degrees earned—figures that, once again, don't auger well for the nation's leadership role in the world economy.

Undeniably and Unacceptably Off Course

Taken as a whole, the nation's academic progress is falling far short of what everyone agrees is needed for American students in the future. This is especially true for black and Hispanic students who have traditionally suffered the disadvantages of poverty, discrimination, and assignment to the weakest public schools in the nation. But it is also true for white students.

As the United States struggles to make small gains, the world is not standing still economically—or academically. America's slow and uneven progress, as measured by its own national assessments, has translated into little or no improvement on international ones. To be sure, there are signs of progress: the rise in NAEP math scores, for instance, and the performance of America's fourth graders on the TIMMS science test. But even these signs are questionable—and meantime, other countries are improving. By and large, the United States has done little more than maintain its midpack ranking against the rest of the world, a bit better for younger students and a bit worse for older students.

The evidence is clear. The United States is not on course to raise its academic standing in the world. Student achievement is far from where it needs to be, progress has been sluggish—and any effort to understand this nation's future, and certainly to do anything about it, must come to terms with what has become a persistent problem of educational performance. What accounts for the slow pace of improvement? Why hasn't the nation been able to shift into a higher gear?

3

THE POLITICS OF BLOCKING

That the nation has an education problem is no secret. Presidents and members of Congress know it. Governors and state legislators know it. Ordinary citizens know it. And the seriousness of the problem—for personal lives, for economic growth, for the nation's status as a world leader—has made education reform a full-time occupation of government. Year in and year out, policy makers have made education a priority and feverishly pushed for new policies and resources to boost student achievement. The sheer outpouring of activity is impressive. It just hasn't succeeded.

The reasons have to do with politics. The key decisions about public schools are made within the political process, and the problem, as we will explain, is that the politics of education is inherently biased toward the status quo. This bias comes about because powerful groups have a stake in protecting traditional arrangements and resisting change—and as the nation pursues reform, they are often able to block. As a result, many good reforms never make it through the political process, and the "reforms" that do are either weak versions of the real thing or are essentially just retreads of the past, unable to bring significant achievement gains.

Technology can be of enormous benefit in the quest to improve student learning. We will see why in the next chapter. But for now, it is important to get perspective on what technology is up against. The fact that it offers enormous benefits is not enough to guarantee that it will be embraced by the public schools and its potential fully realized. Technological change will run into the same political roadblocks that all major reforms have run into, and for exactly the same reasons. Powerful groups will try to block it. As we look ahead and try to get a sense of where American education is headed, this political reality needs to be firmly understood. Technology is the force for change. Get ready to meet the counterforce.

Power and the Politics of Education

The single most important thing to know about the politics of education is that the teachers unions—the National Education Association (NEA), the American Federation of Teachers (AFT), and their state and local affiliates—are extraordinarily powerful, so much so that they are in a different league from other groups with an interest in public schooling. Some readers may be inclined to dismiss this statement as an ideological broadside against the unions. But that would be a mistake. The preeminent power of the teachers unions is a simple fact, and anyone who ignores it or pretends otherwise will misunderstand the politics of education.[1]

The power equation was different in the past. During the first half of the 1900s, administrators—school superintendents, mainly—were the leaders of public education, and teachers had very little clout. Within the hierarchy of schools, teachers were atomized subordinates who lacked any organized means of taking action on their own behalf. The same was true in politics. Many teachers belonged to the NEA, which was indeed powerful, but the NEA was not really their organization. It was a professional association controlled by school administrators.[2]

All of this changed dramatically in the 1960s and 1970s when states began changing their laws to permit collective bargaining for public employees. In education, the AFT got the jump on the NEA—which was initially anti-union—by launching an aggressive campaign in the early 1960s to organize teachers. Faced with do-or-die competition, the NEA quickly morphed into a labor union to meet the threat, and a period of tumultuous conflict ensued. When the dust had cleared by 1980 or so, virtually all school districts of any size (outside the South) had been organized, and collective bargaining and unionization had become the norm. In the process, administrators lost control of the NEA, as well as their leadership of public education. The teachers unions now reigned supreme.[3]

The result was a new kind of education system: similar in appearance to the traditional one, but different in its leadership and distribution of power.[4] Born of teacher revolution, it has been in equilibrium now for a quarter century. Within it, the teachers unions are more powerful than the administrators ever were, for the sources of their power are perfectly suited to the hardball world of American politics. By gaining collective bargaining rights within school districts, the unions have amassed huge memberships—the NEA currently has more than three million members, the AFT more than one million—and tremendous financial resources, mostly from member dues.[5]

The money allows them to contribute generously to electoral campaigns at all levels of government; indeed, in the vast majority of states they are among the top five contributors to political candidates, and in many states they are the number one contributor.[6] Perhaps even more important, their members are located in virtually every political district in the country, where activists ring doorbells, make phone calls, distribute literature, and in countless other ways campaign for favored candidates. Between elections, moreover, the teachers unions exercise power in the legislative process through well-financed lobbying organizations, and they are also active in administrative arenas and the courts.[7]

Throughout American society and across policy areas, few other interest groups can claim this kind of political clout. Indeed, a long-running study of state-level politics found the teachers unions to be the single most powerful interest group *in the entire country* throughout the 1990s, and in 2002 ranked them a close second behind general business organizations (which are only episodically involved in educational issues).[8]

Over the last several decades, this capacity has been developed to a fine organizational art, and in elections is marshaled almost entirely on behalf of Democrats. Such partisanship makes sense, of course, because the Democrats' longtime support of government programs, spending, taxes, and unions makes them the obvious political partner by comparison with Republicans. And when push comes to shove in the policy process, this partnership pays off, for most Democrats—sometimes out of genuine agreement, but always in recognition of the sheer power the unions can wield—are sensitive and responsive to what the teachers unions want on educational issues, and they vote accordingly.[9]

On occasion, the teachers unions back Republicans too. They may contribute to key Republican legislators, for example, in a state where Republicans control the legislature, or they may contribute to relatively union-friendly candidates in Republican primaries to try to knock off Republican incumbents they especially oppose.[10] But these are exceptions. The fact is, more than 90 percent of their campaign contributions go to Democrats. As anyone familiar with American party politics knows, the teachers unions are core members—hugely important and influential core members—of the Democratic political coalition. They and the Democrats are allies.

Many other interest groups are involved in the politics of education too. They just tend to be a lot less powerful. Parents, for example, are chronically unorganized and weak. Many do belong to local PTAs, but these are parent-*teacher* organizations, and research shows they almost never oppose the teachers unions.[11] Virtually all other groups of relevance—business groups, community groups, ethnic groups, religious groups—are not focused on education.[12] They have broader social and economic concerns, and only under special conditions—in times of crisis or deep frustration, say—do they become motivated and active on education matters. The unions are strikingly different. They have vested interests in public education, are totally focused on educational issues, and have every reason to be intensely and continuously active in politics. Most of the time, then, especially when their organization, money, and activists are added into the equation, the unions have huge advantages over everyone else.

Although the teachers unions stand out as unusually powerful, they are otherwise just like other interest groups: they use their power to promote their own interests. These interests arise from the primordial fact that, in order to survive and prosper as organizations, the unions need to attract and retain members, get resources (dues, political contributions) from them, and maintain internal solidarity and support. The specifics take familiar forms. They have an interest in protecting member jobs. They have an interest in fighting for higher salaries, more valuable health and retirement benefits, and better working conditions. They have an interest in pressing for reduced class sizes and other means of increasing the demand for teachers. They have an interest in fighting for bigger budgets and higher taxes. And so on.[13]

None of this has anything to do with what is best for children, at least directly. It is possible, of course, that some union objectives—higher spending and smaller classes, for example—are actually good for kids. Yet research suggests that, if these factors do have a connection to student achievement, it tends to be weak.[14] We shouldn't expect the positives from union activity to be substantial anyway, for they are the accidental by-products of what the unions do in their own self-interest. It is quite clear, however, that self-interest often leads them to do things that are *not* good for kids, such as protecting the jobs of incompetent teachers, refusing to allow veteran teachers to be tested for their substantive knowledge, and insisting on seniority-based transfer rights that make it difficult for administrators to put the right teachers in the right schools and classrooms.[15] The unions don't do these things because they are malevolent. They do them because they are normal organizations guided by their own interests—and because these interests are simply different from, and not aligned with, the interests of kids.

How, then, do they pursue these interests in politics? They do it in two ways: by pressuring for the policies they want and by trying to block the policies they don't want. In practice, however, these are not equally attractive options. The reason is that policy making takes place within a system of checks and balances, whose effect is to make new legislation very difficult to achieve. Typically, a bill must make it past subcommittees, committees, and floor votes in each house; it must be approved in identical form by each; it is threatened along the way by various parliamentary roadblocks (such as filibusters, holds, and voting rules); even if it passes, it can be vetoed by the executive; and even if signed by the executive and made law, it can be challenged and overturned in the courts.

To get a policy it wants, then, a group must win victories at each and every step along the way, which is quite difficult. To block a policy it opposes, on the other hand, it needs to succeed at just *one* of the many veto points along the way, which is a much easier challenge to meet. The American political system is literally designed, therefore, to make blocking—and thus preserving the status quo—far easier than taking positive action. The advantage always goes to interest groups that want to keep things the way they are.

And so it is in education. The teachers unions are extraordinarily powerful, but enacting their favored policies is difficult even for them. More often than not, especially when the policies they seek are consequential for lots of other interest groups—as is the case, for instance, with spending proposals—the unions find that much must be compromised away. Their efforts can be stunningly effective, however, when their sole aim is to block proposals they dislike—because not only do all blockers have a decided advantage, but the unions' massive power magnifies that advantage many times over, making it quite likely that they can stop or water down any reforms that threaten their interests. And which reforms are these likely to be? They include virtually all reforms that attempt to make fundamental changes to the system, for any major reform is likely to unsettle the jobs, security, autonomy, or working conditions of teachers—and to be threatening.

Taken together, these basic elements coalesce to give a distinctive structure to the modern politics of education. For the first time in its history, the American education system has a powerful protector—the teachers unions—capable of shielding it from the unsettling forces of reform and change. As the unchallenged leaders of public education, the unions have amassed formidable power rooted in collective bargaining and electoral politics. They have fundamental interests—interests not aligned with those of children—that drive them to oppose almost all consequential changes in the educational status quo. And they operate in a political system that is literally built to make it easy for them to block.

Mainstream Reform

In the wake of A Nation at Risk, the driving force for change came from business groups and state governors. Deeply concerned about a faltering economy and the growing threat of international competition, business groups saw a mediocre education system as a big part of the problem. They demanded action, and found allies in the nation's governors—whose voters expected them to "do something" to meet the challenge. But what to do? Not experts themselves, governors turned to experts within the education community and set up countless commissions and task forces. All around them, moreover, were high-profile reports by prominent national organizations—the Carnegie Forum on Education and the Economy, the Holmes Group, the Twentieth Century Fund, and others—arguing the need for specific lines of reform, and for urgency.[16]

The ideas that gained the most traction were decidedly mainstream: the schools could be improved by spending more money, adopting a more rigorous curriculum, boosting teacher quality, and making other incremental changes that fit comfortably within the existing system. As a result, the education tsunami that swept across America in the early years after *A Nation at Risk* involved little that was threatening to the teachers unions. When threatening ideas did emerge—this was, after all, a tumultuous time—the unions were largely successful at blocking them. But for the most part, mainstream reform was quite compatible with their interests, and they supported it.[17]

National spending on public education shot up dramatically. From 1982–83 through 1989–90, per-pupil spending increased a full 74 percent—providing the schools, after inflation, with 35 percent more money for every student. Over the following decade, per-pupil spending (adjusted for inflation) increased by another 14 percent.[18] The problem with this spending strategy, however, is that there was never any credible basis for it—no evidence that more money would lead to significant achievement gains—but every reason to believe that an unproductive system would take the additional money and spend it unproductively. Which is what has happened in the years since.[19]

Strengthening the curriculum was a far better idea. Students clearly need challenging course work if they are to achieve at high levels. But this line of reform didn't work either. What the political process yielded was not academic rigor, but the appearance of rigor: stricter formal requirements ensuring that more students would take higher-level courses. Over the 1982–83 to 1989–90 period, graduating seniors did indeed amass more credits in English, math, science, and foreign languages, and they took classes that were supposedly more advanced.[20] It is not enough, however, to give courses impressive-sounding titles, or to force students to sit through more academic classes, unless there is a system of accountability to assure that the content is actually being taught and learned—which, of course, there wasn't. Writing in 1991, in what is perhaps the best historical overview of the early period of reform, Thomas Toch observed that the "vast majority of high school students ... are getting little more exposure to rigorous course work than they did previously. Despite the reformers' successful push for new graduation requirements, [students] are receiving an academic education in name only."[21]

Efforts to improve teacher quality were also a disappointment. This goal surely ought to be a top priority for the nation, for teacher quality is the single most important school-level determinant of student achievement. Efforts by reformers to increase the quality of teachers, however, were another matter entirely, because they quickly got tangled up with the certification, evaluation, and job security of teachers—and came face-to-face with the teachers unions. The unions were in favor of higher teacher quality too, but wanted it pursued (and still do) in circumscribed ways: mainly through stricter certification requirements, better training of teachers in education schools, and the additional training of veteran teachers during their careers—via professional development, college credits, master's degrees.[22] The evidence suggests that these approaches don't work. The ed schools do a poor job of training teachers, formal certification has little to do with student achievement, and the same can be said of professional development, college credits, and master's degrees.[23] But nonetheless, these approaches to teacher quality proliferated during the 1980s—and are the dominant approaches today—because the political gates have been open to them.

For other paths to teacher quality, the unions have shut the gates. It is painfully obvious, for instance, that teacher quality could be improved if the dismissal of mediocre and incompetent teachers were easier to accomplish—instead of being virtually impossible.[24] Yet the unions are in the business of protecting the jobs of all their members, and they are adamantly opposed to reforms that might allow administrators to remove even the most poorly performing teachers from the classroom.[25] Their political success has been so great and so consistent that ideas for modifying the ironclad job security of teachers rarely even make it onto the political agenda for discussion. This was true in the 1980s, and it is still true—as Governor Arnold Schwarzenegger of California discovered when he tried to modify the state's teacher tenure law in 2005: the teachers union led the charge against him, and he and his proposal went down to a crushing defeat.[26]

Another simple way to increase teacher quality is to test all veteran teachers for competence in the subjects that they teach. Clearly, if a math teacher doesn't know math, she can't possibly be an effective teacher.[27] But the unions have stridently opposed such testing, arguing that all teachers with formal certification are competent to teach. During the mid-1980s, new laws requiring the testing of veteran teachers were actually adopted in Arkansas, Texas, and Georgia—states with relatively weak unions—but even in these cases, the tests were purposely pitched at such a low level that they barely weeded out the illiterate, if that, and they quickly fell into disuse. North Carolina adopted a testing plan in 1997 for veteran teachers in its lowest-performing schools, and Pennsylvania adopted a plan in 2001 for testing all its veteran teachers; but within a few years, both were no longer operating. Everywhere else, the unions were successful at blocking even such pathetic attempts to assure substantive competence, and in most states the testing idea has simply been kept off the agenda.[28]

Yet another obvious reform is pay for performance. If teacher pay were to depend (just in part) on performance in the classroom, good teachers could be paid more than bad ones. By rewarding productive behavior, such a system would then do two things: it would give teachers strong incentives to perform at high levels, and it would generate a dynamic of "selective attraction" in which high-quality people would be more attracted to teaching—knowing they will be rewarded for their productivity—and low-quality people would be less attracted and less likely to stay. Both would operate to raise the average quality of the teacher pool.[29]

But the unions want teacher pay to have nothing to do with how well they perform in the classroom, and thus with how much their students actually learn.[30] In their eyes, such a system would create jealousies among members, undermine solidarity, increase uncertainty, and expand administrative discretion—all of which they seek to avoid. What they prefer is a world of professional sameness: in which all teachers with the same experience and educational credentials are paid the same (under the "single salary schedule") and see themselves as doing the same job and having the same interests. Because of the unions' power, this is more than a preference. During the 1980s and 1990s, pay for performance was actively discussed as a policy option—indeed, it was proposed in A Nation at Risk and a number of subsequent reports—but it went nowhere. The unions regularly used their political power to block it, and to push instead for across-the-board raises for all teachers, arguing that higher pay for everyone will attract better people. Then and since, this is the approach policy makers have routinely followed.[31]

Although the reformist pressure behind pay for performance has picked up considerably in the last decade, the unions continue to fight it—so far with great success.[32] As a result, the American education system has been unable to use pay as an effective tool for boosting teacher quality. Good teachers and bad teachers are paid the same. Performance incentives are weak. Selection effects work in exactly the wrong way: with high-quality people turned off by a profession that doesn't reward productivity, and low-quality people finding it a good deal. And across-the-board pay raises—which are extraordinarily expensive, and can't possibly be very large—do nothing to change any of this. They simply perpetuate the sameness.

For all the hullabaloo about a revolutionary era of school improvement, then, the reforms triggered by A Nation at Risk really didn't amount to much. And by the end of the 1980s there was widespread agreement that these early efforts had failed. This realization—and its attendant frustration—led to a surge in support for two major movements that soon took on lives of their own: the choice movement and the accountability movement, which we will shortly discuss. Even with the rise of these new political forces, however, policy makers continued to invest heavily in mainstream reforms. Indeed, as parts of the above discussion suggest, the reforms they pursued during the 1990s—and to the present day—have often been the very *same* kinds of reforms they pursued during the 1980s. Over this entire period, the states have persisted in seeking to improve their schools through more spending, higher across-the-board salaries, stricter academic requirements, more teacher training, and the like—all with great fanfare, as though this time around these recycled efforts will pay off.

Some "new" reforms have gained support and attention along the way. Of these, the most popular is class size reduction, which was heavily promoted by President Clinton via his effort to fund one hundred thousand new teachers for the public schools, and aggressively pursued in a number of states as well: notably in California, which was the pioneer in 1996, and in Florida, where voters in 2002 passed a statewide initiative requiring drastic reductions in class size.[33] Needless to say, this is a reform the teachers unions strongly support. Teachers like it, and it can only be carried out by hiring lots more of them. But the fact is, class size reduction, like the others, does nothing to restructure the system, and there is no evidence that it works to bring about big improvements in student learning, especially beyond the first few years of school. Worse, it is hugely expensive.[34]

Why, over the last quarter century, have the states invested so heavily in reforms with so little promise? The answer is that, despite their ineffectiveness, these reforms are politically attractive. They sit well with common sense, and are thus popular with the public; they also make sense to the business community; and the teachers unions either support them or find them innocuous—and so don't try to block them. From a political standpoint, mainstream reforms are all pluses and no minuses. The only downside is that they don't work.

Accountability

The greatest achievement of *A Nation at Risk* is not that it generated countless education reforms. Most of them have been a waste of time and money. Its greatest achievement is that it directed attention to the problems of public education, put power behind the cause of reform, and gave impetus to the movements for accountability and choice, both of which have the capacity to transform American education for the better.

The ideas behind school accountability have obvious merit. If the school system is to promote academic excellence, it must have clear standards defining what students need to know. It must engage in testing to measure how well the standards are being met. And it must hold students, teachers, and administrators accountable for results—and give them incentives to do their very best—by attaching consequences to outcomes.[35] Writ large, these are simply the principles of effective management that business leaders live by every day: setting goals, measuring performance, attaching consequences, and creating strong incentives.

As the 1980s drew to a close, and as the first wave of incremental reforms proved impotent, accountability offered an approach that promised to get at fundamentals. Moreover, because it was a top-down approach—a demand for effective management that business leaders, governors, and the general public could readily understand—it came across as a natural extension of mainstream efforts to make the existing system work better. It was a reform that everyone could agree was desirable.[36]

Well, almost everyone. The teachers unions and their education allies had a very different view. For the goal of this reform was to hold *them* (or their members) accountable—and this they did not want. Historically, teachers and (most) administrators have been granted substantial autonomy, and their pay and jobs have been almost totally secure regardless of their performance. Why would they want to have specific goals thrust upon them, their performance seriously evaluated, their pay linked to performance, and their jobs made less secure?

With accountability so broadly popular, however, and so much power arrayed behind it, the unions and their allies were in a political bind. Full-fledged opposition would have put them on the wrong side, and pegged them as self-interested defenders of the status quo. This being so, they opted for a more sophisticated course of action: to "support" accountability, participate in its design—and try to block or water down any components they found threatening.

In the years since, the unions have largely displayed their "support" for accountability by embracing the need for curriculum standards. Indeed, the AFT has positioned itself as a leading proponent.[37] But the unions have little to fear from the standards themselves, as long as the latter are not accompanied by serious testing regimes and real consequences for poor performance. So it is the tests and the consequences that the unions have tried to block, or at least weaken and render ineffectual.

Standardized tests have been used for many decades in American education to measure what students are learning. Traditionally, test results were not used to evaluate schools or teachers, were not made public, and usually did not even have consequences for students. The accountability movement has tried to change all this—against union opposition. Publicly, the unions say they "support" testing, but the reality is that they rarely come across a real-world test they like. When the state of Massachusetts instituted a high-stakes accountability test in 2000 for high school graduation, for example, the Massachusetts Teachers Association launched a $600,000 advertising campaign to undermine its public support, calling it "flawed and unfair" and encouraging citizens to "Say no to the MCAS graduation requirement."[38] This is but a dramatic version of what has been happening all across the country for years. In general, teachers unions disparage standardized tests as inadequate measures of student or school performance, and call instead for broader criteria—course grades, portfolios of student work, graduation rates, parental involvement, and more—that would make assessments far more flexible, complicated, and subjective, and much less dependent on objective measures of how much students are actually learning. Needless to say, they are also totally opposed to using standardized tests to evaluate the performance of teachers themselves.[39]

The unions' prime goal is to see that testing does not lead to any sanctions for poor performance. Above all else, they want to ensure that no one ever loses a job, and that there is no weeding-out process by which the school system rids itself of mediocre teachers. Other kinds of economic sanctions, such as school closings or reconstitution, are forbidden as well.[40] Here is a simple example that speaks volumes. In New York City, Mayor Michael Bloomberg and Chancellor Joel Klein, both strong proponents of accountability, attempted a sensible reform of the teacher tenure process. Their idea was to use student test scores to arrive at objective measures of how well new teachers were performing in the classroom, and then to bring this information to bear (along with much other relevant information) when teachers were being evaluated for tenure. The idea that data on student learning should be relevant to teacher tenure seems woefully obvious. Who could disagree? The United Federation of Teachers could, and did. The union took its case to the state legislature, and succeeded in getting a new law passed that flat-out *prohibited* any district in the state from using student test scores in the tenure evaluations of teachers. The information is available. It just can't be taken into account.[41]

The teachers unions are not the only groups that have fought to weaken school accountability. They are joined by many administrators, school boards, and members of the education community who are unhappy about the new requirements; by some civil rights groups concerned that testing may lead to high failure and dropout rates among minorities (although other groups speaking for disadvantaged kids—Education Trust, for example—have come out as strong supporters of accountability); by disaffected parents who think their kids are being over-tested; and by a small army of experts who claim that tests are misleading and biased. Even so, the unions are the eight-hundred-pound gorillas of the anti-accountability coalition, and their political power is the key to its success in weakening the efficacy of reform.[42]

Because the stars have lined up just right—popularity with the public, powerful support from business, leadership by political executives—the unions and their allies have not been able to block accountability reforms entirely. Accountability systems of some sort were adopted in most states during the 1990s. And these efforts were followed by the movement's single biggest victory: the watershed No Child Left Behind Act (NCLB), passed by Congress in 2002, which created an accountability framework for the nation as a whole.[43]

The fact is, however, that these accountability systems are not really designed to hold teachers and administrators accountable. The devil is in the details—in the specific standards and rules that make up each piece of legislation, along with how they are enforced on the ground. Part of the problem is that, with policies as complex as these, even the best-intentioned designers have a hard time creating systems that work effectively from the get-go. Problems inevitably arise, and they need to be worked out over time. This is the case, for example, with No Child Left Behind itself: some of its provisions could surely be improved upon.[44]

But the flaws in accountability systems are not just well-intentioned mistakes. They also arise because their very designs are influenced by the unions and their allies, who do not want educators held accountable. The unions' influence varies from state to state—they are weaker in the South than in the rest of the country, for instance, which is why some of the pioneering efforts in accountability have come from states like Texas, North Carolina, and Kentucky. Their influence also tends to be weaker at the federal level than at the state level; national politics attracts interest groups in far greater numbers, politicians have larger, more diverse constituencies, and the unions have much more competition.

It was due to this relative disadvantage at the national level, plus the fact that the stars happened to line up just right for reformers—a very unusual event, with even top Democrats on board—that the unions lost control of the politics of No Child Left Behind. They were unable to block it. They also failed in their efforts to deflate many of its key features, such as its strict reliance on standardized test scores in evaluating the "adequate yearly progress" of schools. Even so, they scored important victories—notably, in eliminating private school vouchers for kids in failing schools, and in eviscerating the requirement that veteran teachers demonstrate competence in their subject matters (which has led, years hence, to the charade of virtually every one of the nation's three million teachers being declared "highly qualified"). More generally, their power succeeded in keeping NCLB within bounds, and almost devoid of serious consequences that would actually be enforced on the ground.[45]

As things now stand, this nation has fifty-one different accountability systems, one for each state and the District of Columbia, which conform to the NCLB framework but have their own standards, their own tests, and their own sets of consequences and enforcement actions.[46] Although these systems vary considerably, it is generally the case that:

- There are no mechanisms for weeding out mediocre teachers. Teachers continue to get paid and have totally secure jobs regardless of how much their students learn.
- Data on student performance are not put to systematic use in measuring teacher performance.
- Teacher pay continues to follow the traditional salary schedule and is not linked in any way to how much students learn.
- Schools rarely suffer any sanctions—reconstitution, transfer of students, and the like—for failing to teach their children.

The list could go on. These are accountability systems that do something positive: they put the focus on student achievement, provide objective measures of performance, encourage public discussion about how the schools are doing, and put more pressure on them to improve. But they are also inherently defective, because they fail to include mechanisms that are pivotal to their effective operation. And the reason they fail to include these mechanisms is that they were designed under the influence of their enemies—who "support" accountability systems that don't in fact hold anyone accountable.[47]

Design is just the beginning. Because the battle never ends. The NEA, for example, is currently fighting No Child Left Behind in the courts, attempting to have it declared illegal—and thus to block it after the fact.[48] Both the NEA and the AFT have been fully engaged in the political struggle over the reauthorization of No Child Left Behind, pushing for modifications that would give it even fewer teeth, opposing efforts to include measures—such as pay for performance—intended to make it more consequential, and hoping to have its reauthorization blocked altogether. And both unions are actively involved in public relations campaigns that loudly criticize accountability—students are over-tested, teachers are teaching to the test, pay for performance is "a blatant attack on collective bargaining,"[49] and so on—in efforts to convince the American public that accountability is a bad thing.[50]

There is nothing radical about accountability. It is a reform that simply makes sense, and that business leaders take for granted as an essential component of any effective organization. Were it not for the influence of unions and their allies, accountability would be a more serious undertaking in the public schools too. And the focus would be on making schools work for children, instead of protecting the jobs and work privileges of adults.

School Choice

School choice has provoked more political conflict than any other education reform, accountability included. On the surface, this might seem perplexing. Choice would simply allow families to choose their own schools, and thus, most important, to leave failing schools for better ones: an option especially valuable for those who are poor and minority, because they are often stuck in the nation's worst schools. Precisely because families could leave for better options, moreover, all schools would be put on notice that, if they don't do their jobs well, they are likely to lose children and resources—consequences that would give them incentives to perform and innovate.[51]

To the unions, however, choice is deeply threatening. Were parents able to seek out other options—notably, charter schools and (with vouchers) private schools—the regular public schools would have smaller enrollments. They would provide fewer jobs. They would control and disburse less money. They would be under more pressure to produce. And the unions would lose members, resources—and power. So there can be no surprise that they are intensely opposed to school choice, and have long been engaged in political efforts to block it.

The unions are the vanguard of the opposition, spending most of the money and mobilizing most of the troops. But they have important allies. The NAACP has little faith in markets, and has long seen choice as a veiled opportunity for whites to flee blacks. It is also concerned about job protection: urban school systems are a prime source of minority jobs, and these jobs would be threatened if kids were given the freedom to leave. The ACLU and People for the American Way are mainly concerned about the separation of church and state, seeing vouchers for private schools (many of them religious) as a dangerous breach in the "wall of separation." Liberals in general tend to be supportive of government, suspicious of markets, and worried that the poor cannot make good choices for themselves. And Democratic elected officials—pivotal to the enactment of policy—tend to be liberal, electorally dependent on the teachers unions, and usually willing to support them on key issues.[52]

Choice was first proposed in the mid-1950s by conservative economist Milton Friedman and later promoted by Ronald Reagan. In the realm of American education, though, conservatism and market-based arguments were no match for the blocking power of the union-led coalition. Nor, stereotypes aside, could school choice count on the political clout of business to even the balance, for the fact is that people in business tend to see education reform in managerial terms. Management is what they do for a living, and in their eyes it is the key to effective organization. Support for accountability flows naturally from this orientation—but support for school choice does not.

Without a power base in business, the choice movement has lacked the concentrated political punch of the accountability movement. It has gained a modicum of success, though, by taking a left-hand turn from its libertarian roots. The signal event came in 1990 when parents in inner-city Milwaukee, where the public schools were abysmally bad, rose up to demand vouchers as a means of escaping to better options in the private sector—and were vigorously opposed by the teachers unions and their allies. The political lineup couldn't have been more potently symbolic: the teachers unions unleashed their full arsenal of weapons to prevent poor parents from getting their kids out of failing schools. By entering into a coalition with conservatives, however, the urban poor won a surprising victory. It was a limited one: a pilot program in which no more than one thousand disadvantaged kids could qualify for vouchers, and religious schools were disallowed. But the choice movement got a huge boost—and the nation got its first voucher program.[53]

Since 1990, choice advocates have focused most of their reform efforts on poor and minority families in the inner cities. The modern arguments for vouchers have less to do with free markets than with social equity. They also have less to do with theory than with common sense. It seems pretty obvious that disadvantaged kids should never be forced to attend failing schools—ruining their prospects for productive careers and futures —and that they should be given immediate opportunities to seek out better options.

This shift toward equity has expanded the constituency for choice, with polls consistently showing that its greatest supporters are poor and minority parents. Nonetheless, the opponents have been quite successful over the years at blocking. When supporters have put choice proposals on the ballot, the unions have poured millions of dollars into advertising campaigns to convince voters that vouchers will destroy the public schools, leading in each case (there have been ten of them, going back about twenty years) to defeats for choice.[54] The unions' bread and butter, however, has been in the state legislatures and the U.S. Congress, the forums in which the nation's key education policies are designed and adopted—where the unions have done a masterful job, year after year, of preventing voucher proposals from becoming law.[55]

Despite all the blocking, choice advocates have managed to eke out victories here and there. They won major expansions of the Milwaukee program. They won several new voucher programs: for low-income children (Cleveland, Washington, D.C.), for kids in low-performing schools (Florida, Ohio, Colorado), for kids in special education (Florida, Arizona, Utah, Georgia, Ohio), and even for all kids statewide (Utah). And they also enacted several programs that, through tax credits and nonprofit foundations, provide scholarships for disadvantaged children (Arizona, Florida, Iowa, Pennsylvania, Rhode Island).[56]

But as with accountability, the battle is never over. The unions target each victory and doggedly try to overturn it. They overturned the Utah program, after its adoption by the legislature, by putting it on the ballot and spending heavily (aided by $3 million from the national NEA) to defeat it.[57] They also got state courts to invalidate the Colorado voucher program, one of the three Florida voucher programs, and the Arizona programs for special-needs and foster kids.[58] For many years, moreover, they pursued court challenges to the Milwaukee and Cleveland programs—both of which eventually survived. The Cleveland case was ultimately heard by the U.S. Supreme Court, resulting in the landmark Zelman decision in 2002, which ruled that including religious schools in a voucher program is constitutional.[59] This case was a loss for the unions. But a victory would have struck a serious blow to the choice movement. And by simply launching these and other court actions—there have been many—they keep voucher programs in a continual state of uncertainty, making it difficult for the programs to attract parents and become established.

The voucher programs that remain have to be considered impressive victories, given the opposition. Even so, they are unimpressive as crucibles for significant change. There are more than fifty million public school students in this country, and only a little over one hundred thousand children are receiving publicly funded vouchers or tax-credit scholarships (of varying amounts, sometimes small)[60]—a total that hardly makes a dent in the public school population and, outside of Milwaukee (where close to twenty thousand kids now use vouchers[61]), offers little competition to help improve the public schools. The bottom line is that the opponents have been extremely successful at preventing the spread of vouchers.

Reformers have also fought hard for charter schools, which provide choice within the public sector. Charters are *public* schools of choice, but they are independent of district control and free of most regulations that burden the regular public schools. The idea is that charters will give families more options to choose from—especially important in urban areas, where many schools are low performers—and that competition will stimulate the regular public schools to change their ways and improve, so as not to lose kids and money.[62]

The choice movement is in a much stronger political position on charters than vouchers. Many Democratic officials, well aware that disadvantaged children are often stuck in bad schools, see choice as a way to provide them with new, more attractive options. Because of their own ideological inclinations, and because the unions are so fiercely opposed, they cannot (now) support vouchers. So charter schools give them a middle ground: they can support more public-sector choice for disadvantaged families while still opposing vouchers. Thus, the choice movement has found it much easier to pick up Democratic allies in pushing for charter schools, and much easier to win.[63]

From the unions' standpoint, however, charters are threatening. Charters allow money, students, and teachers to leave the regular public schools. And they are typically nonunion and not covered by the collective bargaining contract. Still, because charters are part of the public sector—and thus more vulnerable to legislative and district (and therefore union) efforts to control them than are private schools—the unions do not put charters in the same league as vouchers when drawing up their must-block lists. They have tried to salvage their public image, as well as give their Democratic allies some wiggle room, by following a more accommodationist strategy.[64]

By no means is this always their approach. When a philanthropist offered to put up $200 million of his own money to fund fifteen charter schools in the city of Detroit, for instance, the teachers union went on the warpath to prevent it from happening—launching a fierce political fight in the state legislature, sending thousands of teachers to demonstrate outside the capitol, and eventually getting their way. The $200 million was turned down. The charters were not created.[65] In many other cases, however, the unions' strategy has been to "support" the concept of charters, and then—if blocking isn't a feasible or attractive option—to push hard for key restrictions in the legislation. Among them: extremely low ceilings on the number of charters allowed statewide, lower per-pupil funding than in the regular public schools, districts as the sole chartering authorities (because the districts don't want competition, and have incentives to refuse), no charter access to district buildings, requirements that charters be covered by union contracts, and, in general, the imposition of as many of the usual state and district rules and regulations as possible—to make charters just like the regular public schools.[66]

For these reasons, most charter systems are inherently limited. And this is not the end of it, because the politics of opposition never stops. Once these programs are in place, the unions continue to try to unsettle them and bring them down. One line of attack is through public relations: they generate a stream of claims and studies arguing that charter schools do not improve student achievement, aiming to shrink the popularity of charters and defuse the movement. The most "successful" of these studies—carried out by the AFT's own staff—actually wound up on the front page of the *New York Times*.[67]

Another standard line of attack is through the courts. The unions have gone this route in many states that have enacted charter legislation—New York, New Jersey, Minnesota, and others—usually arguing that charter schools violate state constitutions, and that the new legislation should be annulled. But perhaps the most telling example comes from Ohio, because in this state the charge was led by Tom Mooney, president of the Ohio Federation of Teachers (OFT), who was also a founding member of the Teachers Union Reform Network (TURN), an organization of union leaders who consider themselves reformers, and who say they support an enlightened unionism that strives to do what is best for children.[68] Yet in 2001 Mooney and the OFT filed a high-profile court challenge in state court to have Ohio's charter school system declared unconstitutional, and accompanied their court case with a public relations campaign to discredit charters as poor performers. Ultimately, they lost: the Ohio Supreme Court ruled against them in 2006.[69] But this was hardly the end of the system's legal troubles. In 2004, well before this case was decided, the Ohio Education Association (OEA)—the other state teachers union—filed suit in federal court, claiming that charter funding was unfair and violated the due process clause of the fourteenth amendment to the U.S. Constitution. Then in 2007 the OEA filed suit in state court seeking to end the diversion of funds away from traditional public schools to charters.[70] (This suit was later dropped when the state's Democratic Attorney General announced he would launch his own legal attack on charters.[71])

Despite all the conflict and struggle, the charter movement has clearly made progress. Charters have become the most widely accepted approach to school choice in American education. As of 2008, forty states and the District of Columbia have adopted laws authorizing the creation of charter schools, and there are more than four thousand of these schools in operation, enrolling roughly 1.3 million children. These are big numbers that far exceed the successes of voucher-based reforms. On the other hand, they pale by comparison to the ninety-five thousand regular public schools and fifty million public school students. So although charters have in some sense swept the nation, the fact is that the political process has kept the lid on this reform quite securely, and except in certain urban areas—twelve cities had more than twenty percent of their kids in charter schools in 2007–08, led by New Orleans at 55 percent (due to the Katrina disaster) and Washington, D.C. at 31 percent—it has prevented the movement from taking wing and promoting fundamental change.[72] For the most part, today's charter systems offer very little choice and very little competition. And even so, they are under continual attack.

Privatization is another target of union power. Many reformers believe that school districts or chartering agencies should be able to contract with private firms to operate failing public schools, so as to take advantage of the expertise, efficiency, and innovation the marketplace might offer. This is only reasonable. If it succeeds, great—the students are better off. If it doesn't, the contracts can be terminated. But here again, the unions are threatened: the last thing they want is for privatization to work well, become widely adopted, and create an outflow of jobs and money to the private sector.[73] And with the unions thus opposed, privatization has been blocked in all but a small percentage of the nation's school districts. The most successful private provider is EdisonLearning, which operates seventy-five schools around the country—a tiny number, needless to say, given the huge population of public schools.[74]

Even when these firms manage to be hired, moreover, they are in for a heap of trouble. The local unions typically just keep on fighting: making claims about the firms' "poor" performance, inciting teacher and parent opposition, accusing firms of doctoring test scores, pursuing court cases to challenge the firms' authority and decisions, and otherwise making privatization a miserable, costly, and politically tumultuous experience for all concerned—hoping that the practice of contracting out will be discredited, that contracts will be terminated, and that firms will be scared out of the business.[75]

Despite the suffocating effects of union power, market-based reforms have slowly moved ahead over the last few decades. Choice, competition, and privatization are taken seriously in today's policy arenas, there is real (if often inadequate) power behind them, and they have established a beachhead in American education. As with accountability, however, there is more symbol than substance here. For even when these reforms have "won," the unions have succeeded in imposing all manner of restrictions and limitations to ensure that there is actually little choice, little competition, little reliance on market dynamics—and little threat to their interests. What appear to be revolutionary reforms are mostly gutted by the time they make it through the political process.

Blocking the Future

The politics of education is hardly a shining example of democracy in action. On the surface, it may seem vibrant and pluralistic. There are, after all, countless groups and public officials involved, and there is flowery rhetoric about solving education problems and doing what's best "for the kids." But most of this is misleading. For beneath the complex action and soaring symbolism, there is a very simple structure at work: the politics of blocking.

The building blocks of this structure are rooted in a few basic facts of political life. It is a fact that the teachers unions have vested interests in preserving the existing education system, regardless of how poorly it performs. It is a fact that they are more powerful—by far—than any other groups involved in the politics of education. And it is a fact that in a government of checks and balances they can use their power to block or weaken most reforms they do not like. To recognize as much is not to launch ideological attacks against the unions. It is simply to recognize the political world as it is.

Because the politics of blocking is very real, and because it has long kept the lid on American education reform, the challenge of *A Nation at Risk* has gone unmet. Major reforms—accountability, choice—that attempt to address the fundamentals of poor performance and inject strong, performance-based incentives into the heart of the system have been resisted and undermined at every turn. And even the simplest, most straightforward attempts to target the school-level determinants of student achievement—efforts to boost teacher quality, for instance—have run into a wall of obstruction.

After a quarter century of reform, the nation has made scant progress. Indeed, most of its reforms are not worthy of the name. Its accountability and choice systems are too weak to do their jobs well, and are under constant attacks intended to weaken them further. And the mainstream reforms that make up most of what the policy process produces—more spending, across-the-board pay raises, more teacher training, reductions in class size—have little impact on student achievement, but a lot to do with why the American school system becomes more and more expensive without gaining in productivity.

What, then, about the information revolution? If we ignore politics it is easy to believe that the sheer enormity of technological change, combined with the vast educational benefits it holds for children, will surely lead to a transformation of the American school system: to greater customization, more diversity, more choice, and all sorts of innovative changes that we can only begin to imagine in today's world. Yet politics cannot be ignored. And if anything is stone-cold certain about the current structure of power, it is that technological change is destined to be resisted by the teachers unions and their allies. This is "their" system, and they are compelled by their own interests to preserve and protect it. They will go to the ramparts to see that technology does *not* have real transformative effects. They will try to block.

4

TECHNOLOGY ON ALL FRONTS

In 1986 Midland, Pennsylvania, a small steel town near the Ohio border, was forced to close its high school. A few years earlier, the Crucible Steel Mill had shut down, leaving this once thriving community of less than five thousand in dire economic straits. Residents began exiting in search of jobs, the tax base eroded, and a high school for only a hundred students became financially untenable. Midland kept its elementary and middle schools going, but for the next decade worked with nearby towns to provide a high school education for their kids. None of the arrangements proved satisfactory—in fact, a neighboring school once rejected Midland students because its local quarterback lost his starting job to a boy from Midland. In 1990 Midland negotiated with East Liverpool, Ohio, to provide a high school. But that arrangement raised hackles all the way to the state capitol in Harrisburg, as Pennsylvania tax dollars were leaving the state to pay for public education. A better solution was clearly needed.[1]

In 1995 Midland hired the son of a former steelworker as its superintendent. Dr. Nick Trombetta had never run a school district, but he brought to the job a special sense of mission. As a teacher, coach, and administrator in various school systems around Midland, he had witnessed the steady erosion of a once proud way of life for Eastern European immigrants, like his parents, tied to steel and related industries. He had watched as local schools declined with the economy—posting some of the lowest scores in the state and serving increasingly impoverished and diverse families. So when Midland offered him the helm of its struggling school system, Trombetta had no specific plan, just a conviction that for the families that had stuck it out in Midland and for the sons and daughters of working-class families like his, he would make a difference.

His first objective was to do something for the perpetually displaced local teens without a high school. Fortuitously, Pennsylvania had just authorized charter schools in 1997. State officials had been working with Midland to find a high school solution that did not send kids to Ohio. They suggested to Trombetta that perhaps the charter law could provide a solution. At the same time, Trombetta's board wondered whether emerging online education technologies might be part of the solution. Blending the two, Trombetta and his board decided to try to create a cyber charter school. Trombetta knew little or nothing about high-tech education or charter schools, but being entrepreneurial by nature, he decided to take a closer look. Over the next couple of years, he and several longtime colleagues assembled a modest plan. Local educators would design the courses, and with no need to pay for facilities or maintain traditional teacher-student ratios, a cyber high school would be something that Midland could afford.

The plan was for the Western Pennsylvania Cyber Charter School, as Midland named its school, to open with fifty local students in the fall of 2000. To Midland's surprise, over five hundred students from all over the state enrolled during the first year. In 2004 U.S. Senator Rick Santorum chose the school for his own kids. Test scores rose steadily. Today, PA Cyber, as it is known—"Western" was dropped from the school's name—serves upwards of eight thousand students. The school and affiliated entities provide eight hundred jobs in the local community, mostly teachers and curriculum developers. The old steel mill headquarters, home to the former bosses, is bursting with instructors working with kids on the Internet. The local economy is recovering nicely. Nick Trombetta and little Midland created the largest virtual charter school in the nation.

Cyber Charter Schools

Technology is beginning to transform instruction. As it does, it will transform schooling as we know it. Online courses and cyberschools are the most dramatic manifestation, as they take students completely out of traditional classrooms and brick-and-mortar schools. Indeed, the motto of PA Cyber is "Build Your Own School—Out of Choices, Not Bricks."[2] In 2005–06, seven hundred thousand students in kindergarten through twelfth grade took courses online—about 1.5 percent of students overall.[3] For perspective, that is already more than a tenth of the total number of students enrolled in private schools nationwide, and the online enrollment was built in less than a decade. Cyberschools are growing rapidly by providing opportunities not available in traditional schools. Sometimes their services are welcomed by traditional school systems—for example, when they serve dropouts—but mostly they are fought tooth and nail. We devote the entire next chapter to the politics and resistance surrounding their creation and growth. Here we want to focus on education and the innovations in schooling that online instruction make possible—and likely, irresistible.

In 2002 Ray Rozycki was chairman of the math department at South Fayette High School in McDonald, Pennsylvania, about twenty miles from Midland. Today he is the chief academic officer of Provost Systems, a technology firm based in Santa Clara, California, that designs tools necessary to deliver online learning in K–12 schools. Rozycki was one of the local teachers recruited by Nick Trombetta to create courses for PA Cyber. He was a rapidly rising star as a math teacher and was named chair of his department at a young age. Otherwise, he had no experience preparing him for high-tech course design. But he had something else going for him. He knew the students he would be designing for—kids just like those he was teaching at South Fayette—and he felt responsible for their success. Collaborating with colleagues whom he handpicked for their success in traditional classrooms,

Rozycki began working in his spare time to design the school's second generation of online math offerings. (The school concluded that the first generation, only three years old, could be improved upon. It was learning its new business quickly.) Over the next several years Rozycki and growing numbers of local educators—and in time, professional writers and software developers—created an online program that works well for both students and teachers. In May 2007 Rozycki joined the school's primary software developer, Provost, full-time.

We focus on Rozycki and the development of the PA Cyber model because they illustrate how technology can empower educators to do things for students that they would otherwise never dream of accomplishing. Just as technology has empowered countless individuals around the globe—all one needs is a laptop and an Internet connection to try entrepreneurship—so will it empower educators. The experience of Rozycki, Trombetta, and their colleagues also illustrates how swiftly innovations can emerge in an online environment through the dynamic interplay of students, parents, teachers, and software designers. PA Cyber developed many important innovations in instruction and, with Provost, in technology as well—all to meet the demands of parents and students. The school did not attract thousands of students without quickly learning lessons, making adjustments, and offering an improving product that kept students signing up in increasing numbers. This kind of dynamism does not exist in the traditional public education system.

When PA Cyber launched, it built its courses on a technology platform designed for colleges and universities by a company known as Blackboard. Online learning has already become a huge business for higher education and the companies that support it. Every college and university now has to have online offerings or lose students to other institutions. Online learning is a $6.2 billion enterprise for higher education and its business partners.[4] Blackboard dominates the market for online learning platforms, and the platform works exceedingly well for higher education.

In 2007, 20 percent of all postsecondary degrees included some amount of online credits.[5]

But the Blackboard platform was not ideal for high school and certainly not for middle or elementary education. It did not allow for alignment of course content with state standards. It did not provide for easy communication with parents. It did not readily keep track of student work to gauge persistence. Its student information system did not allow reporting to multiple entities—namely, the many home school districts of students enrolling statewide. It did not offer interfaces that were attractive to younger students. Most important, it did not offer a range of instructional tools that would help engage, motivate, and ultimately help precollegiate students to learn. The college-level platform was very good at presenting professors' lectures and textbook-like materials, but not at using technology in more creative ways. PA Cyber was experiencing the effects of the law of supply and demand. Because K–12 education, unlike higher education, has been noncompetitive and resistant to online instruction, technology companies and publishers that serve traditional school districts have produced little to help fledgling cyberschools.

PA Cyber therefore had to invent and improvise—as have all of the online charter and online state schools. This is a good thing and characteristic of dynamic markets. Provost was a small technology consulting firm started by a young California entrepreneur, Anthony Kim. He had gotten his feet wet with online instruction while doing related work for California colleges and universities. He created Provost with contracts from those institutions to customize the Blackboard platform for them. PA Cyber contacted Provost when it found that Blackboard was out of synch with its virtually unique—at the time—education needs. Together, they went on to create a host of software products explicitly suited to online schools: an alternative platform for launching courses correlated with state standards, a student information system that manages student records and assessment data from a multitude of school districts and facilitates communication with far-flung parents, a gradebook tailored to assignments that may or may not involve teachers, and much more. They created an assessment engine that generates randomized exam questions, so that students taking tests at their own pace couldn't give fellow students a heads-up via e-mail. (Yes, it happens; cyberschools become virtual communities with online networking.) The technological innovations, which came fast and furious, created in just a few years a whole suite of tools for delivering K–12 education online and giving students and parents a seamless experience of attending a virtual school—and not merely taking random courses online. Ray Rozycki—whom Kim asked to join Provost in 2007—and his teaching colleagues drove these innovations as they worked to ensure that their kids, and then thousands of others, would succeed.

More important than the technological innovations were the instructional ones. Courses were all built on a common template so that students would have a similar experience regardless of the subject being taught. The educators designing the courses quickly learned that if students were going to persist through courses—and PA Cyber has a 95 percent completion rate—the courses must be comfortably familiar and intuitive to navigate. Some online systems, many operated by states, have admixtures of courses and instructional designs that kids often struggle to comprehend—"electronic correspondence schools," Nick Trombetta calls them. In sharp contrast, every PA Cyber course is consistently structured and makes innovative use of technology. Each course is a semester long, divided into four units, with ten lessons per unit. Each is scored on a thousand-point system. The points earn course grades, but they also earn online incentives. Students have personal "avatars," much like in a video game, to navigate course problem sets and exercises. Points that students earn from their performance on exams, homework, and other assessments can be used to customize the avatar—something young people find very engaging. The courses make ample use of video and animation to help students understand the material.

Lest one think that PA Cyber turned education into some sort of video game, it is important to understand that PA Cyber courses make significant use of live educators. And students are generally provided with a textbook—all materials shipped in a handy package right to the home—to supplement what is delivered online. Teaching staff are differentiated creatively. Every student is assigned a faculty adviser who is responsible for monitoring student progress, ensuring that the student is devoting enough time to course work and making reasonable progress. The adviser is required to communicate with student families at least every week by e-mail and every two weeks by phone. Each adviser works with 80–120 students. This is more counseling support than students receive in traditional schools.

Online teachers are of two types, synchronous and asynchronous. Synchronous teachers work with students in real time, while they are online engaged with their lessons. The teachers communicate with students by instant messaging, voice, and interactive whiteboards. Synchronous teachers answer student questions and help students better understand material presented electronically or in their texts, novels, or other traditional course materials. Synchronous teachers are especially important for children with special needs or otherwise in need of greater support. They work with fifteen to twenty-five students in elementary or middle school and up to thirty per class in high school, ratios similar to brick-and-mortar schools—but students can access teachers for one-on-one tutoring at any time. Students can choose which courses they want to take with teachers synchronously and asynchronously. On average, students have taken about a third of their courses synchronously—the choice generally depends on how strong a given student is in a particular subject.[6]

The synchronous instructors are supported by asynchronous teachers who focus on grading. They read student essays, term papers, research projects, and other assignments, and provide written feedback. Assessment methods at PA Cyber are as diverse as in any quality school. Multiple-choice questions and other test items, efficiently administered electronically, are but one part of the assessment process. Asynchronous teachers are committed to twenty-four-hour turnaround—which is fast by traditional standards. They work full- and part-time (many of the part-timers are teachers in brick-and-mortar schools during the day), and they work effectively with large numbers of students—two hundred or more per semester.

PA Cyber serves nearly eight thousand students in grades K–12 with about 230 educators full- and part-time. In its October 2007 annual report to the state, the school noted a student-teacher ratio of 30 to 1, as measured by full-time equivalents.[7] Over twice as efficient as traditional schools in this respect, PA Cyber is able to spend public education dollars differently. In particular, it is able to invest very heavily in course design. Regular school districts invest next to nothing in course design; they buy textbooks and leave course design to teachers. PA Cyber has invested millions of dollars in its courses, and now has a repertoire of 250 courses in all. It is currently in the midst of a multimillion-dollar investment in a curriculum for the primary grades, K–4. Every PA Cyber course is rigorously audited for instructional quality by an affiliate of the University of Pittsburgh, and the public can visit its Web site to see how each course measures up. Traditional school systems do not have the wherewithal to have their courses independently evaluated. The work that PA Cyber and its technology partner, Provost, have done has been so impressive that Stanford University is discussing a partnership with them to augment the university's online high school.

This is all immensely creative. But the key question is, does it work? PA Cyber serves a diverse range of students. Three-fourths of the students are in high school, the toughest grade range for meeting state standards. Students include many who were not successful in their traditional schools and were looking for a second chance. Some were victims of bullying, some were already dropouts. Some were homeschooled children without any evident learning issues. Nearly half of all students are eligible for free or reduced-price lunch, a relatively high percentage for high school students who notoriously underreport their eligibility. The racial makeup of the school is typical of the state's demographics: 86 percent white, 11 percent black, 3 percent Hispanic, Asian, or Native American. In 2006–07, with nearly six thousand students to serve, the school made Adequate Yearly Progress (under NCLB), satisfying twenty-one of twenty-one targets. Across the state, barely half of all high schools made AYP. PA Cyber graduated over seven hundred students in 2007. The SAT average for PA Cyber students was 97 points above the state average.[8] A Stanford University study of PA Cyber documented significant growth by PA Cyber students in reading, math, and writing—indicating that the school's academic performance is at least partly due to its value added.[9] Students could reap these benefits, moreover, regardless of where they lived in the state—a final important difference from traditional public schools.

To be clear, the lesson to be learned here is not that online schooling is a superior method of instruction to traditional schools, or even that it is definitely working. The lesson is that, once freed from traditional school system rules, public education meshed with technology can innovate very swiftly. Teachers can play new roles, lessons can be presented in creative ways not possible in a traditional classroom, students who are poorly served by traditional arrangements—as evident by their voluntary enrollment in an online alternative—can be reached in large numbers. Moneys can be poured into instructional design that would otherwise be spent on teachers who now have to design all courses themselves. This reallocation may be the most important development, equipping a smaller number of teachers with better instructional tools—and perhaps, as we shall show, paying them more. The curriculum of PA Cyber is an impressive creation fueled only by regular public school dollars, not private investment. The curriculum and its creative team were recently spun off into

a not-for-profit organization, the National Network of Digital
Schools, which provides the courses to other schools, school districts, and state education departments. The curriculum is a living
memorial to Midland's long-departed Lincoln Park High School.
It's called "Lincoln Interactive."[10]

The Wide World of Technology

If Midland, Pennsylvania, seems an unlikely place for a technological revolution in the United States, Gurgaon, India, might be
the least likely place on the planet for a tech uprising. The streets
are clogged with tens of thousands of rusty bicycles, busted rick-
shaws, and aging miniature cars. Beggar women still press their
babies to car windows looking for a handout, despite a national
law that has outlawed begging since 1959. The roads are lined
with shanties and settlements that provide some of the poorest
housing in the world. Mountains of roadside rubble and trash are
grazed by cows—holy in India—as well as dogs, pigs, goats, and
other homeless animals hungry for food. Men regularly relieve
themselves in public.[11]

But there are two faces to Gurgaon. Amid the grinding poverty, magnificent business towers are sprouting rapidly to the sky.
The largest turnpike interchange in the world—thirty-two lanes
wide—collects tolls from the hundreds of thousands of cars speed-
ing daily between Delhi, the nation's capital, and Gurgaon on
a new superhighway. When the interchange opened in January
2008 it created forty-minute delays because traffic had already
eclipsed planners' estimates by 20 percent. A massive monorail
system connecting the two cities is being constructed at break-
neck speed. Every major name in the technology world can be
found on the glimmering walls of the new high-rises—Microsoft,
Dell, Oracle, IBM. For every office buzzing with activity—at rush
hour thousands upon thousands pour out onto to the dusty local
roads—there is another office under construction.

Gurgaon is an exemplar of the rapid transformation of India.
Since the introduction of stable democracy twenty years ago,

India has been making up for lost economic time. With a culture that values education, a labor force that provides high levels of skill at very low prices—the supply simply outstrips the demand many times over—and a government that is friendly to business and entrepreneurship, India has become the favored partner of Western firms looking for major efficiencies in their operations. Back-office functions in Western companies have been moving rapidly to India for some time. Help desks now routinely employ Indians to service customers in the United States and throughout the Western world. India's economy is booming as a result—growing over 9 percent annually, and for the last quarter century at twice the rate of the Western world during the industrial revolution. Despite its grinding poverty, India now has between two hundred and three hundred million citizens enjoying middle-class standards of living, and 1 percent of the poor join the middle class every year.[12]

In 1994, Santanu Prakash, a recent business school graduate with no money but a keen eye for entrepreneurship and a bold vision for education, started a little company in Gargaon. Prakash recognized the almost unimaginable challenge that is Indian education. The public schools in India—950,000 of them in all—have struggled for years with crowding and limited funding. Classes routinely include forty-five students. Teachers are poorly paid. The vast majority have no formal certification, and their commitment to their work is uneven at best. Absenteeism among teachers is a widespread problem with daily rates as high as 70 percent. The middle class tends to shun the government schools in favor of some fifty thousand private schools. But with very modest tuitions—sometimes only $10 per month—they have trouble attracting strong teachers; even amid today's affluence, a private school teacher typically earns only $10,000 per year.[13]

Prakash had the straightforward insight that technology might offer an answer to the issue of teacher quality. Over the next decade, he and his growing team created an interactive computer-based curriculum delivery system that totally changes the role of the teacher. Every classroom is equipped with a large flat-screen monitor. On either side are whiteboards. The monitor is connected to a school server that contains literally all of the lessons for every subject taught in the school, kindergarten through twelfth grade. The content employs animation, video, dramatization, and every available presentation option to deliver complete lessons in every classroom. Teachers play the role of facilitator, pausing the presentation to ask questions and prompt critical thinking. The whiteboard allows for direct intervention in the lessons. The pedagogy is not passive video watching; it is quite interactive, blending teacher and technology. But the technology relieves the burden on teachers to prepare content-based presentations for every lesson in every subject every day. In the 2007–08 school year, the system—known as *Smart Class*—was being used by three million public school students and one million private school students in a total of six thousand schools. Schools have been adopting the system so rapidly that Prakash's company, Educomp, is doubling in size every year.

Educomp employs over a thousand Indians in and around Gargaon and is contributing to the rapid growth of the Indian middle class. Low wage costs and growing numbers of engineers, programmers, scientists, and other professionals are making India a major partner and competitor in the development of technology worldwide. These advantages are likely to persist and indeed even strengthen in years to come because of the sheer size of the Indian population striving to enter the middle class. Education is but another field where India's comparative advantages will make it a driver of technological innovation.

Already, hundreds of thousands of students around the world are being tutored by Indian teachers online.[14] Working for a fraction of the wages of teachers in the United States and Europe, Indian firms are leading the pack in developing technologies that can provide families with personalized and affordable help with their schoolwork at home. For years, tutoring was only available to families that could afford to pay private tutors—such as those who work for companies like Sylvan and Huntington—the high going rate for face-to-face sessions in costly brick-and-mortar tutoring locations. With tutoring now moving online, using some of the same technologies as online schooling, tutoring is becoming more affordable and convenient for many more families. Traditional U.S. tutoring firms, and new ones such as Tutor.com, are moving online. But they operate at a huge disadvantage to Indian firms that can provide a high-quality service for a much lower cost. Yes, the Indians must be carefully trained to speak with less native accent and to understand teen colloquialisms in the United States and Europe. But just as help desks in so many industries are now staffed by or run by Indians, so too—the smart money says—will tutoring services for Western kids.

As the market for home tutoring grows, with its affordable rates for average families, something important and unexpected happens. Yes, kids get valuable extra help with their schoolwork. But the business of high-tech education gets a surprising boost. As we have noted, the public education system—in the United States and many other Western democracies—has a strong tendency to resist innovations that might threaten the status quo. This is especially true of the United States, where blocking is so readily available as a political strategy, and where threats to jobs—such as low-cost online tutoring—are at the top of union lists of things to block. If education technology firms had to sell only to public education systems, sales would be slow and innovations that even remotely threatened jobs or wages would not be encouraged. The family-pay market offers an important difference. It provides firms the incentive to invest in online education solutions and to demonstrate their merits without the constraints of breaking into the establishment market.[15] The online tutoring market is growing 15 percent annually in the United States, with Indian firms leading the way, either alone or in partnership with U.S. firms needing low-cost, high-quality tutors.[16]

India and other countries with low wages and rising education levels—China is Exhibit A—have other advantages over the West. As Educomp's success illustrates, India and others have vast education needs. Most of their populations are semiliterate and living in poverty. They also have education systems that are patently failing and cannot effectively resist change. They have teaching workforces that are themselves poorly educated. If technology offers a way to provide better instruction to kids, the systems are in no position to resist it. With a huge domestic market, Indian firms can contemplate investments that may not pay large margins school by school, but that promise enormous revenues nonetheless.

Educomp offers another example. Over the last couple of years it developed the largest education portal in all of India. Known as *Mathguru.com*, the Web site offers audio and whiteboard solutions to every problem in every math textbook used in India. If a student is struggling with his or her homework, the Web site provides a ready lesson, complete with step-by-step explanations. Educomp developed the Web site on its own technology platform. A similar platform has been under development in the United States, created by Academy 123, a start-up outside Los Angeles. It was recently purchased by the Discovery Channel, and is slowly getting to market. In 2006, Educomp approached Academy 123 about a partnership to license their new platform. But when Academy 123—then in the midst of being purchased by Discovery—said it needed ninety days to evaluate the prospective deal, Educomp said, "We can develop a platform ourselves in ninety days." And they did.

The economics of educational technology investments are different in India and countries like it than they are in the United States and other Western nations. Costs of developing new technologies are dramatically lower—perhaps only a tenth. Domestic markets are much larger. The education establishment is much needier and less resistant to change. All of this creates very fertile ground for innovation, and for spending what it takes to try out very different ideas. The products that Educomp has created would not have been created at all, or as fast, if it were a U.S. firm. The United States should expect to see these products, proven abroad, coming to our shores whether the establishment welcomes them or not. The first customers may be parents, Internet advertisers, dropouts, or students in cyber charter schools.[17] But more and more, the education world will have to face opportunities and challenges from all around the world.

The power of technology today simply cannot be overstated. It is being developed in every corner of the world, by firms that have minimal costs, huge markets, and little resistance to their work. But the drivers behind technology are becoming even more powerful than these. Much of what technology brings to the education table has no cost at all. Students, parents, and educators interacting online create new knowledge every day. Teachers participate in online professional learning communities that may help them become more successful—interacting with colleagues in real time—than traditional workshops or college courses. Students already interact online on *Facebook* and *MySpace* at rates that have made these two Web sites among the ten most visited in the world, and this was accomplished in less than five years of existence. Although most of the interaction by students is social, the potential for supporting learning is huge. Web sites already attempt to structure online social networking for educational value—for example, through "wikis" such as *Schoolwork.ugh!* (www.schoolwork.org), which dispenses homework advice. And speaking of wikis, the father (or mother) of them all, *Wikipedia*, has become the encyclopedia of the millennial generation, built over time from the contributions of millions of users—for free.

Among technology developers, and some developers of education content online, the vision of the future is all free. At least when it comes to the direct cost of usage, technology platforms and educational material will often be free. Just as anyone can create a Web site or a wiki or a blog these days, in the future more and more platforms for communication and interaction will be available for free. The business models that support such "open source" approaches to technology platforms and information sharing are obviously not based on returns from keeping information or resources scarce.[18] Businesses will find it profitable to share some intellectual property for free, in order to drive customers to more valuable goods or services for which they are willing to pay. Already much of the Internet works this way. It is easy to imagine a time when textbooks and other print resources will be available at no cost on the Internet, but online personal tutoring, to support the materials, will require payment. More fundamentally, free access to content and technology online will further accelerate the pace of innovation, as potential participants face no costs to contribute.

As technology picks up the pace, education will face unbearable pressure to adapt and improve through technology—a pressure that almost every other industry in the world has already faced. Initially, of course, the educational system will resist. Technology promises to change the fundamentals of how teaching and learning have taken place for centuries. But as education solutions prove themselves in every arena—including (eventually) the traditional classroom—to be patently more effective and more efficient than the status quo, the resistance will prove counterproductive. Adapters will be more successful than resisters. Technology will become integral to public education, not peripheral to it.

Technology and Instruction in Brick-and-Mortar Schools

The evidence of a technological revolution is unmistakable in cyberschools, the international education arena, and the world of social networks. But change is also apparent, if comparatively glacial, in brick-and-mortar schools. This is to be expected given the deeply institutionalized nature of public education and the politics of blocking that sustain the status quo. But important, even fundamental shifts are occurring that presage greater movement down the road, particularly as traditional schools face competition from cyber charters using technology far more creatively. The most obvious of the coming changes are in information systems, as we discuss below. But instruction in traditional schools is beginning to evolve as well, and the potential even for transformation is becoming clear.

It begins with access. In 1998 the average public school had one computer connected to the Internet for every 12.1 students, which translates to about two computers per classroom. Just seven years later, in 2005, the ratio had fallen to one Internet-connected computer for every 3.8 students, a threefold improvement.[19] By that same year, 94 percent of all public school classrooms were connected to the Internet, up from only 51 percent in 1998.[20] Today classroom access to the Internet is near 100 percent. The investment in connectivity has been fueled by the federal E-rate program, which has poured about $2 billion per year into public schools since 1998.[21] A 1999 survey of technology use in public schools found that one of the main reasons technology was not used frequently for instruction was a lack of computers.[22] Today, this is simply not the issue.

The issue is usage. It would be hard to find anyone knowledgeable about technology in schools who would argue it is yet having a major impact on instruction. Elliot Soloway, a professor of computer science and education at the University of Michigan, and someone who has devoted his career to developing computer applications for the classroom, summed it up bluntly: "The honest assessment is [technology] has had very little impact."[23] Students use computers more outside of school than within it. Young people are "digital natives." They know nothing but a world of instantaneous technology—except in the schoolhouse. Outside school, students use laptops, cell phones, MP3 players, and an ever-changing array of devices to communicate and access information and resources. Their purposes may be mostly for socializing and entertainment, but the technological experience is more sophisticated than what they typically have at school. In a recent book on teens and technology, *Totally Wired*, Anastasia Goodstein observes that technology use at schools is dominated by teacher presentations using PowerPoint and student research using the Internet. Students do not master even the basic productivity tools, such as spreadsheets, and they do not make much use of electronic programs that instruct.[24]

Why the slow pace of innovation? It is not a lack of ideas. In the 2007–08 school year public education spent a total of roughly $25 billion on educational materials and technological supports, from textbooks to computing hardware and software to enterprise systems to outsourced tutoring and management services.[25] Roughly 20 percent of that spending was on computing hardware and another 20 percent on supplementary instructional programs, most of which are delivered electronically.[26] In all, that's a major share of education's external dollars devoted directly or indirectly to uses of technology. By business standards the amount that public education spends on hardware and software is small—less than 2 percent of education's nearly $500 billion cost. But what is being spent has generated a host of educationally innovative technology applications to support core instruction.

Unlike online courses that aim to provide the full content of a traditional class, supplementary programs aim to fill instructional niches. With greater intensity and specificity, they develop skills that students may not grasp fully in a regular classroom. They offer animation and other visual demonstrations that convey ideas differently than what a classroom teacher can provide. They allow instruction to be customized to the needs of the student. They teach skills, such as foreign languages, that regular schools may not be able to afford to provide with live teachers—and they sometimes do it with no teachers at all. Dozens of these programs now exist, and with documented records of achievement. Remedial math and reading programs are the most common. But these programs run the gamut of subjects.

A particularly ingenious online program, Achieve 3000, illustrates the unique potential of technology.[27] A challenge that teachers routinely face in teaching any subject that requires students to read—history, civics, or science, for instance—is that students in the same class often have widely varying reading levels.

Teachers quickly find that holding a class discussion or asking students to analyze or write about something they have read is undermined by diverse abilities to read. Poor readers never get to show their content knowledge or thinking ability because the written material may be too difficult. Strong readers may be bored by reading material that is too elementary or may become distracted as teachers use class time to assist the stragglers. *Achieve 3000* corrects this problem by offering an online library of readings about a host of specific topics, written at every reading level from first grade through high school. More remarkably, the staff at *Achieve 3000* writes sets of multiple-grade-level readings about current events *every day*, and posts them on their Web site every evening. Schools can have discussions of truly current events that every student in a class can readily comprehend. The program can be used in this fashion to support traditional teachers, or it can be used without teachers, as students interact with grade-appropriate readings and test their wits with computerized exercises and assessments. This kind of real-time curriculum and customized instruction would be impossible without technology. It brings benefits to students that traditional classrooms simply cannot.

Examples of technology's unique benefits abound. Reading comprehension is a problem for two-thirds of American students, as we saw in Chapter Two. For many of these students the issue stems from a failure during the primary years to gain fluency—the ability to decode letters and sounds quickly, automatically, and unconsciously into words, phrases, and sentences. Without fluency, students cannot comprehend complex text because the sheer concentration required to decode leaves little mental capacity to think about what is being read. Ideally, schools would catch and remediate these fluency problems during the primary years, before they cripple comprehension. But fixing fluency requires attention to individual decoding issues and lots and lots of practice. Instructional programs have been created to accomplish this, through instruction in very small groups. But this is expensive—requiring lots of teachers—and time consuming.

In recent years, technology has provided promising solutions that appear superior to teacher-led approaches.

Programs with brand names, such as Lexia for primary students and Soliloquy for older students, have proven track records of effectively facilitating the decoding and fluency skills so critical to comprehension.[28] Students work on computers with headphones and microphones, reading and listening, and carrying out exercises that enable them to work on the skills that are their individual weaknesses. Even small-group tutorials could not match the level of individualization or the frequency of individual practice that the computer offers. Plus the on-screen presentations, with highlighted text and animated exercises, are engaging in ways that only technology can be.

Tens of millions of American students can benefit from this kind of reading instruction. Similar programs, such as ALEKS, provide individualized instruction in math, and the frequent practice necessary to develop automaticity.[29] Every student needs to reach a point where reading and math fundamentals are second nature—and every student can benefit from what these technologies have to offer. But some students require even more specialized support to acquire the basics of reading and math. Students with special needs, with learning disabilities, may have challenges in processing information that are more basic than even decoding. They may, for example, have difficulty distinguishing subtle differences in sound. Neuroscientists have identified this issue and technologists have developed software for helping train the brain to make these distinctions. Fast ForWord is the brand name of one such product.[30] Used in thousands of schools since the late 1990s, the program is one of the most thoroughly researched instructional technologies on the market, and—as documented by the federal *What Works Clearinghouse*—has helped tens of thousands of special needs and low-achieving students read.[31]

Neuroscience is gaining insight into how learning occurs, and these insights are being translated into new instructional software. These discoveries and innovations will steadily improve their academic efficacy. To be clear, technology is not some sort of educational panacea. Technology-based instructional programs have been used in schools for nearly twenty-five years. Some widely used programs—such as "integrated learning systems" popular in the 1980s and early 1990s—proved of uneven value at best. But technologies have improved very rapidly in recent years, and the Internet has opened whole new avenues for technology and instruction. It matters little that technology has much to prove about its effectiveness at this juncture.[32] In the highly competitive world market in which educational technology is being developed, ineffective products are quickly weeded out and new, more effective products are being introduced daily. There is every reason to believe that technology will only become more effective with time. The same cannot be said of the traditional "technology" of education—teachers and classrooms—unless that world changes fundamentally.

Customization, Teacher Quality, and Hope from Hybrid Schools

Scores of technology-based instructional programs are being used in schools throughout America. They are sold by lots of small entrepreneurial firms, as well as by the big three textbook publishers: Pearson, McGraw-Hill, and Houghton-Mifflin. In fact, it would be rare to find a school that is not using some software package or online service to provide remediation. Federal Title I dollars often pay for them. But the consequences for students, teachers, and schools are currently quite modest. The reason is that technology simply does not mesh well with the long-established organization of schools and classrooms. This is the heart of the matter. A recent survey indicated that the two main issues holding back technology use are "It doesn't fit in the schedule," and "There is not sufficient time to train teachers." Nowhere does it say that the software is inadequate or that technology has dubious instructional value.[33]

Schools are organized today to deliver instruction by traditional means: textbooks, blackboards, and teachers. The politics of education, dominated by teacher unions, has long reinforced the model—making schools ever more labor intensive, relentlessly pushing down class sizes, and keeping students in classrooms led by teachers. The structure being what it is, technology can fit into the schools in basically two ways. It can support the teacher in the traditional classroom, à la PowerPoint, or it can be offered directly to students—for example, by assigning them time in a computer lab, usually supervised by an instructional technology specialist. Neither approach makes adequate use of technology.

In the classroom, students are really not using technology. The teacher is. If every student had a laptop computer, of course, students could participate as well. Someday, one-to-one computer access may come about, particularly as handheld devices gain in power and drop in price. But schools would currently have to increase computer access fourfold to reach that level—a major and ongoing investment. The computer lab is the most common opportunity for student computing in schools today. But its instructional value is severely limited by the lack of integration of the lab instruction with what is happening in the classroom. Teachers drop their students off at the lab while they take their contractually guaranteed planning period. A school technology specialist supervises the lab, and the students do what the computer tells them to do. When the teacher picks the students up at the end of the lab experience, regular instruction resumes with the teacher having little idea what the kids have learned and continuing with a very non-tech curriculum.

Of course, some teachers and schools work hard at integrating technology tools and traditional tools in an effective mix of pedagogy for students. They will, for example, use mobile carts of laptops to bring computing into the regular classroom instead of the isolated lab. But in general, integration does not happen. Schools are simply not organized for instruction to be anything but teacher led. Habit and politics have kept it this way.

But this will not last forever. More effective ways of organizing schools and instruction are becoming obvious, and competition from schools that are not bound by traditional politics will force the laggards to change. What are the opportunities to enhance effectiveness? The most promising involve improving the quality of teachers and allowing students to receive instruction electronically when it is at least as effective as traditional instruction to do so.

The single most important influence on student achievement is teacher quality. Research has demonstrated that a highly effective teacher—one in the top quartile of effectiveness—can raise a student from the lowest quartile of the national achievement distribution to the highest quartile, up to 50 percentiles, in just three years.[34] Schools need to attract higher-quality candidates and then give them better on-the-job opportunities to learn their craft. Better teachers with more time to plan their lessons would make far more effective use of classroom technology than weaker folks who still think that overhead projectors are a technological innovation. Technology offers a ready strategy for building more teaching capacity and offering more time for planning. If students take whole courses online, schools can reduce the number of teachers they require.[35] If students take full advantage of supplementary online programs for skill remediation or acceleration, schools can reduce their need for teachers still further. Students can work in computer labs or library media centers in which multiple classes can readily be accommodated. With parental supervision, older students could do some of their course work at home. But even ignoring the home connection, lab management software now makes it easy for one adult to oversee and direct computer usage by many students. LanSchool, the leading program, allows one teacher to see seventy-five student computer screens on the central management monitor, making sure students are working diligently, and assisting them when necessary—though software does an increasingly impressive job of keeping kids engaged.[36]

If students make more use of technology, the number of teachers required in a school can be reduced significantly. If elementary students spend but one hour a day learning electronically, certified staff could be reduced by a sixth. At the middle school level, two hours a day with computers would reduce staff requirements by a third. High schools, with three hours of usage, could reduce staff by up to a half. This level of computer use is quite feasible given instructional technology that exists today. Imagine the boon in educational technology that would result if more schools moved in this direction and business had incentives to invest much more heavily in online resources. The pace of technological innovation will only quicken as schools become more open to using it.

The quality of teachers would benefit from the increased use of technology in at least two important ways. Even after investing in hardware and software, which are trivial compared to the cost of teachers, schools would have funds from staff savings to increase teacher pay and to provide more time for teacher training and planning. Added time for professional development, with proper supervision and accountability, would improve teacher quality. Added pay would help attract and retain better talent. Better talent is the most important ingredient of better schools.

The Dayton Ohio charter schools that we introduced at the beginning of this book are already demonstrating the feasibility of these ideas—in the toughest of circumstances. Dayton View Academy and Dayton Academy serve students and families in great economic and academic need. Nearly 100 percent of the over sixteen hundred children at these K–8 schools are eligible for free- or reduced-price lunch. Virtually all students are African American, with a community history of very low achievement. When the schools opened in 1999, their initial enrollees averaged only about 25 percent proficient by Ohio standards in reading and math. Over the coming years, the schools improved slowly, implementing a comprehensive reform model emphasizing sound basics: a well-researched core curriculum aligned with state standards, a balance of instructional methodologies, regular formative assessments, and daily professional development to raise teacher quality. It also employed some nontraditional elements, most notably a longer school day and school year. By 2006, achievement had clearly improved: proficiency rates against state standards had roughly doubled at each school and the gains exceeded those of the Dayton public school system.

But the schools were not succeeding as the board had long envisioned. Too many kids were not proficient. State and federal goals were not being met without fail: adequate yearly progress (AYP) was accomplished some years but not others. The board came to believe that further improvement was unlikely without more radical measures. Over the years, two problems consistently stymied achievement. The first was teacher quality. Dayton is unfortunately a community losing industries and jobs. Once venerable businesses like Delco, National Cash Register, and others have closed or downsized. Fresh college graduates interested in teaching are not inclined to teach in Dayton. Whether they attended one of the local university teaching programs and would choose to remain in Dayton, or they matriculated from a teaching program elsewhere in the state or nation and would need to move to Dayton, prospects know that Dayton offers limited economic opportunity for them or, if they are married or thinking about marrying, for a spouse. Veteran teachers are hard to attract and retain as well, either because they are committed to the regular public schools or, like the novices, because they are lured to better economic opportunities elsewhere.

Teacher quality was not the only persistent issue for these charter schools. Students presented another challenge. The vast majority of students came to school with learning deficits rooted in the histories of underachievement in their homes and communities. Little exposure to print material, little experience being read to prior to kindergarten, little reinforcement of standard oral English language, limited encounters with elevated vocabularies outside of school—the classic sources of underachievement. But these problems can be overcome, and Dayton View and Dayton

Academy helped many students do so, some exceedingly well. But as students made progress, they presented a new challenge in classroom after classroom: their achievement levels became increasingly heterogeneous, requiring teachers to work with kids who sometimes varied as much as six grade levels in achievement by third grade. Every teacher struggles to differentiate instruction sufficiently to meet the needs of struggling students who may not yet read and high flyers reading several grade levels above most of the class. Weaker teachers find these disparate levels almost impossible to satisfy. The schools, of course, tried the standard remedies—regrouping classes for reading by level, providing one-on-one tutoring, and special decoding and fluency programs for the poorest readers. Although these measures helped, they were not satisfactory.

In 2007, the schools therefore embraced a radical new approach. They invested heavily in technology to allow them to differentiate instruction on a very large scale. And by substituting technology for teachers, they plowed the financial savings back into teacher compensation to attract and retain stronger teaching staffs. The compensation program included signing bonuses, salaries modestly above market rates, and a bonus program for individual, team, and schoolwide improvements in student achievement on the Ohio Achievement Test. It is too early to tell how much more students will learn through these initiatives, but suffice it to say the early returns are encouraging.

The schools changed roughly 50 percent of their staffs before the opening of the 2007 school year, after rigorous evaluations using qualitative and quantitative measures the previous spring. The schools attracted veteran teachers with records of achievement from neighboring states—a first—using signing bonuses. Novice candidates were asked to provide records of their own academic achievement, including their SAT or ACT scores, because research has shown very clearly that teacher verbal ability is a predictor of teaching success. The schools did not stop their talent search, moreover, when the school year began. Through regular observation in the Fall of 2007, principals quickly identified promising and problematic teachers. In a move truly unusual in public education, the schools made many more staff changes at midyear, getting first crack at new teachers graduating from local universities in December.

Meanwhile, students were being introduced to new high-tech learning venues and instructional programs. There were glitches and bugs. Kindergarten students struggled to simultaneously type "Ctrl-Alt-Delete" to log on to lab PCs. They also routinely lost or forgot their passwords. After a week of tears, they remained in their regular classrooms until the problems could be solved. The venues offered a multitude of instructional technology programs, catering to every grade level from kindergarten through eighth, every learning level, and a variety of subjects. Each program required its own user name and password. Even older students were frustrated by that. Students needed to be assigned the right programs to meet their individual needs. This required painstaking diagnostic assessments of every student by classroom teachers—who are not experienced diagnosticians. The program to accomplish this, AIMSweb, took teachers many weeks to master.[37] Teachers were uncomfortable with the lab management software and with leaving their classes to the supervision of another teacher; the large venues were designed to be supervised by the teacher of one class while the teacher of a second class received a free planning period—meaning sixty students to be supervised at once. The list of challenges goes on.

But six months into the school year, progress is unmistakable. Every student, including kindergarten, now spends sixty to ninety minutes daily in large, technology-supported learning venues learning in *highly customized* fashion. The venues operate very smoothly. In "My Learning Lab" students work in "pods" of six partitioned laptop stations per pod, and ten pods in all—enough computers to support sixty students in the lab at a time. The students enter the lab enthusiastically, sit down at their assigned pods and consult the assignment individually determined by their teacher based on prior diagnostics. Each student quickly logs on and begins work targeted specifically to his or her learning need. In a lab of two third-grade classes, some students will be working, with oral cues and feedback through headphones, on a reading fluency or decoding program. Others may be analyzing current events and self-assessing their comprehension via news articles written at a sixth-grade level. Others may be learning and practicing math skills electronically—gaining instructional insights not possible in a regular classroom and receiving the additional time necessary to master them.

Computers are not the whole customized learning story. A neighboring venue, the Library Media Center, has been overhauled as well. In the middle of the space, under a lowered ceiling known by its free-form shape as "the cloud," students work in a group a bit smaller than a whole class, through lessons led by a teacher using an electronic whiteboard. This high-tech successor to the traditional blackboard allows lesson material to be displayed electronically. More interesting, it permits students and teachers to interact with the screen by touch and allows images, video, and animation to be brought to lessons immediately and effortlessly. Traditional teaching is strengthened and students are more easily engaged. Around the outside of the center, beyond the many bookcases that border the cloud, students are working independently using various media. Some are listening to books with headphones and following the words on the printed page—improving their fluency and comprehension. Others are reading books the old-fashioned way, sitting cozily on giant pillows in a corner. Still others are using a dozen or more computers, again taking advantage of customized instructional programs keyed to their respective needs.

A final oversized instructional venue is the "Flex-Lab." This space is designed for a mix of computer-based instruction and small-group tutorials. Half of the students in the space work on individualized assignments on computers. Half are tutored by a teacher working with a series of small groups. The teacher moves from group to group, again organized by customized need, teaching a mini-lesson, giving students work to do independently, then following up to evaluate progress, answer questions, and reteach.

The striking thing about all these venues, just six months into their operation, is how easily students have adapted to the call to work independently. Part of this is due to the almost inherently engaging nature of technology—kids are experiencing in school the same bright, interactive, multimedia presentations they know so well from computers outside of school. Students are also engaged because the work they are doing precisely meets their needs. They are not frustrated by work above their level or bored by work below their level. Both situations obtain too often in regular classrooms. This point cannot be overstated. Even if students are not using computers in these venues, the instruction is targeted precisely to their needs. With instruction so customized, they are engaged. We emphasize as well that the students in Dayton are by background low achieving. Their learning issues often come with behavioral issues and discipline problems. Yet, supervised generally by only one adult in double-sized classes, these students are engaged and presenting few problems. Customization promotes engagement, which in turn promotes learning.

The operational signs in these Dayton schools are encouraging. Students are spending five to ten times as much of their day learning via technology as students in most public schools. This time is largely devoted to highly differentiated instruction not possible in a traditional classroom. Meanwhile, the traditional classrooms are being taught by a rapidly changing staff, aggressively recruited, rigorously screened, and better compensated to try to raise the level of teacher quality. The basic idea is that better teachers will improve the performance of the core instructional program, whereas technology and other forms of customized instruction will provide effective differentiated instruction to complement the core.

The signs are also encouraging for achievement. Monthly benchmark assessments, which have been delivered electronically to the students in these schools for several years, rose much more sharply during the 2007–08 school year than in any year prior. Scores on the 2008 Ohio Achievement Test generally improved in reading, the subject for which software was introduced earliest. Scores in math were up in some grades and down in others—a reflection of the much later introduction of math technology (in February 2008) and the weak teachers remaining in some grade levels. It is too early to tell how much academic improvement, or lack thereof, was due to technology or teacher quality. The innovations continue to be fine-tuned during the 2008–09 school year, and the board is committed to seeing them through. There is simply no question that better quality teachers and better targeted instruction—which technology certainly provides—will improve student learning.

The innovations in Dayton only hint at how brick-and-mortar schools could change and improve with the spread of technology. They underscore how technology and teaching complement and improve one another. Schools with more technology and fewer teachers are the most likely path of the future. These hybrid schools offer great hope for major improvements in achievement, raising teacher quality and having both technology and teachers do what they each do best. If only brick-and-mortar schools were free to do the same—and had incentives to.

The Power of Information and Transparency

In *The World Is Flat*, Thomas Friedman observes that information is so powerful that it may well have toppled the Berlin Wall.[38] It became increasingly untenable for the Soviet Union to dominate Eastern Europe as modern communication (pre-Internet, even) exposed the economic disparities between the East and the West. In *Complications*, Atul Gawande, a physician and medical writer for *The New Yorker*, explains how patient knowledge of doctor and hospital success rates has transformed medical practice in many fields, encouraging, for example, hyperspecialization.[39]

Many industries have been transformed as technology has made it possible to track core processes and measure performance with great precision. The *Six Sigma* practices pioneered by General Electric to maximize quality have become standard procedure in the most successful firms in private industry.[40] Information drives change.

In education, information has historically been in short supply. This is especially true of information about school performance. Until the early 1990s, systematic data on the outcomes of schooling were rare. Schools were run based on inputs. Buy the right books, hire teachers with the right credentials, schedule students into the right classes with the right number of minutes. Superintendents could cite chapter and verse about what their school systems were doing *for* students; they just had little to say, at least that was reliable, about how much students were learning as a result. The accountability movement that began in the early 1990s sought to do something about this. It said, enough with ensuring schools have the right inputs, let's take a hard look at outputs. So began the then-novel idea of testing students against objective standards to see how schools measured up, and if they were improving.

The accountability movement unleashed a demand for tools that would help school administrators meet the new requirements.[41] Some of this demand was for educational improvements, such as instructional materials and tutoring programs better matched to state tests. Some was for what leaders and managers in any industry now want: better ongoing data on how their organizations are doing. In the early days of the accountability movement, administrators joked that they *prayed* their students had performed well on the day of high-stakes testing; until test results came back months later, they had no idea whether their kids had succeeded or failed, and the Creator was about the only available source of immediate feedback. As the cliché goes, however, hope is not a strategy. But what else could administrators do? There were no reliable data to consult.

In time, school districts tried to create their own measures. They developed tests for teachers to administer once or twice during the school year that supposedly correlated with the actual state test at year's end. The process consumed lots of paper, involved cumbersome scoring and reporting procedures, and used bubble sheet technology at best. It provided information that was neither very timely nor very reliable or valid. But it did have one positive effect. It helped teachers and principals appreciate the importance of at least trying to monitor student progress against state standards.

In the meantime, technology firms were beginning to develop far more sophisticated and powerful information systems for school districts.[42] Businesses had been adopting new systems as technology made rapid improvements. School districts followed suit. They built or acquired programs for administrative data, such as personnel, finance, food service, transportation, procurement, and supply chain management. They installed far more powerful student information systems to address attendance, scheduling, demographics, discipline, and grade reporting, as well as communication with parents. They were handling all of their data far more effectively than ever before—with one exception. Academic data was still poorly tracked. State test scores were distributed to schools and teachers in paper reports. Schools had no way to monitor what was being taught or how students were progressing. At the start of each academic year, schools found it so difficult to distribute test scores from the previous spring to students' new teachers that they did not even try. Teachers began each year ignorant of the strengths and weaknesses their students had displayed on the state tests—tests that would need to be taken again the following spring.

But the pressures of accountability continued. In 2002 No Child Left Behind gave teeth to every state system. School performance would be regularly and systematically measured, and the public would know exactly how its schools were doing.[43] Performance was becoming transparent. A school could not hide the fact that it was achieving less than a neighboring school, that its performance had slipped, or that it was failing kids with special needs. By this time, technology had come far enough to provide solutions. Firms began to develop online "benchmark" assessment systems. Schools could electronically administer tests as often as monthly to gauge student achievement. The tests were written to correlate with, if not mimic, state tests. Benchmark results could be used to predict how each student would fare on the state assessment if it were given at that time. The results also diagnosed student and classroom achievement issues, so that weaknesses could be pinpointed and remediated. The systems were fully electronic, allowing teachers, principals, and students themselves to know precisely where they stood versus the standards for which they were accountable. Since 2002, these formative assessment systems, as they are generally known, have been the fastest-growing segment of the in-school software market, rising 25 percent per year.[44]

Companies with established assessment skill, such as The Princeton Review, became major players in the formative assessment market. They took skills that they had honed in a market long dependent on testing—college admissions—and applied it to the K–12 market. New companies also took up the entrepreneurial opportunity. A new product, AIMSweb, which we saw in use in Dayton's hybrid charter schools, provides fine-grained measures of the most nuanced skills, such as those basic to decoding, fluency, and math automaticity. The probes in this system are designed to be administered as often as weekly, to gauge student progress in specialized skills. It offers data so specific that it converts teaching, for the most struggling students, into a clinical model of individual diagnosis and prescription. As in medicine, learning issues are diagnosed and treated in ways that most closely match the individual's need. Information technology makes all of this possible.

The majority of school districts in America currently have at least basic formative assessment systems. The majority of those, however, are not used effectively. Teachers tend to be uncomfortable having their ongoing success or failure scrutinized so publicly. They complain that the time for administration and analysis takes away valuable time from instruction—the familiar complaint about "overtesting." Even if the tests are administered, it is difficult to get teachers to adjust their instruction accordingly. Schools do not have systems to manage curriculum, support lesson planning, or methodically deploy the right resources in response to issues identified by the data.[45]

Technology firms are now busy trying to help. The latest in academic information tools are curriculum management systems that align instructional resources with state standards, guide and standardize lesson planning for teachers, and serve as repositories of resources for teachers to adjust their instruction on the fly. SchoolNet is the leader in this application, and has been adopted by major school systems including Philadelphia and Chicago—beginning to bring transparency where it has been sorely lacking.[46] Additional tools match online tutorials for students with their benchmark results. Still others offer online professional development keyed to the weaknesses that students demonstrate in each teacher's class. Technology firms are hard at work on the "killer app" (an unbeatable technology application) that will integrate all assessment data, formative and high stakes, with online tutorials and professional development.[47] The ultimate goal is for total integration through what are known as enterprise systems. These would span all of the information needs of a school district. In an ideal world a district's administrative system would be integrated with its student information system, which in turn would be integrated with its academic data system. A district could easily examine, for example, if a spending increase was having an impact on student achievement or discipline, or if teacher performance appraisals correlated with the achievement of their own students. These variables—spending, achievement, discipline, and teacher performance appraisals—now exist in separate databases and are not easily linked.

The pursuit of better data is not being driven by technology firms. It is being driven by school administrators who are accountable for student achievement and are willing to pay to improve the quality of their data. Until very recently, school system data was a notorious mess. It will take time for public schools to have the kind of information about their core processes and outcomes that the best businesses have. But the change is coming with unbelievable speed, and it is likely to accelerate. As information about school performance becomes more widely available, the public will demand more. And the public will demand that practices contributing to performance problems not be tolerated.

The most important example of this will surely be with data on student achievement. With formative assessment systems, principals and district administrators already know who their most effective and least effective teachers are—by watching how benchmark assessment scores improve, classroom by classroom. States are quickly building integrated data warehouses that will give them the capacity to know which teachers statewide are most and least successful. With students now tested at every grade level, 3–8 inclusive, data systems can measure how much value any individual teacher adds to his or her students. Fully integrated data warehouses allow for analytical controls on variables such as student economic disadvantage, race, and ethnicity, and a host of other relevant factors. These analyses must be done carefully, so as not to mislead about school performance or to judge any teacher unfairly. At least one state, Florida, has already completed calculations of teacher effectiveness and offers teacher bonuses to districts that will use the calculations to make awards. Every state will inevitably follow.[48]

Currently, what states and school systems know about student achievement at the level of individual teachers is not publicly available. But as the information comes into existence, the public will demand to know it. Parents will insist that their children be placed with teachers of demonstrated effectiveness. District policies that seem to ignore this valuable information—for example, giving teachers pay increases with no regard to the achievement of their students—will be publicly challenged. Once information is available it cannot be suppressed. It is that powerful.

Consider New York City as a case in point.[49] The New York City Public Schools, with fourteen hundred schools, 1.1 million students, seventy-seven thousand teachers, and another sixty thousand employees has long been among the most bureaucratic school systems in the nation. The teachers union is undeniably powerful, and city politics make progress nearly impossible. In 2001 the city elected a new mayor, Mike Bloomberg, a billionaire businessman, who demanded and won from the state legislature control over the public schools. Until that time, the schools had been controlled by an elected board which in turn appointed the chancellor, or superintendent. Bloomberg hired a Washington lawyer, Joel Klein, as his chancellor, and the two of them set about trying to bring basic business practices of accountability and transparency to the system. The district resisted in predictable fashion. But Bloomberg, Klein, and a courageous new leadership team persisted. In time the schools improved, reversing a generation of poor and stagnating performance. Dropout rates fell and reading and math scores rose substantially. In 2007 the New York City public schools won the coveted Broad Prize in Urban Education, at least one indicator that New York is on a most promising trajectory. Much of this progress could be attributed to the bright light shown by the new administration on school performance.

In 2007 the city took its transparency measures to the next level. Chancellor Klein began implementing an integrated management system known as ARIS, for Assessment Research Innovation System. The system is a product of an $80 million contract with IBM and some of the best assessment minds in the country, including Tom Kane of Harvard University. The system is a fully queriable database that incorporates every imaginable piece of data about schools, teachers, and students. It is being used to estimate teacher effectiveness based on state test scores, with controls for all variables that might also affect achievement.

Like outside research, New York analysts are finding that teacher effectiveness is not well predicted by intake variables such as certification or degrees.[50] It is unobservable except through the value-added assessment of test scores. The teacher effect is huge—half a point on a four-point testing scale when the best teachers are compared to the worst. The district has now incorporated a unique annual calculation of teacher effectiveness for every teacher in the system.

The district aims to use the indicators to make major personnel decisions. Most important, it wants to take tenure decisions out of the hands of principals and base them instead on three years of value-added assessment data. By sorting the wheat from the chaff at tenure time, the district's goal is to slowly but surely upgrade the quality of its teachers. Unfortunately, that goal cannot be met in the near future—for as we discussed in Chapter Three, the teachers union went straight to the New York legislature in protest, and used its political power to engineer new legislation that prevents the city school district (and indeed, all school districts in the state) from using student performance data as a factor (even if one of many) in teacher tenure decisions. So the district is blocked for now. But it is hard to imagine, particularly with the political changes we'll be discussing later on, that objective information on teacher effectiveness will be kept under wraps for very long.

Meantime, the district's information system continues to be valuable for other reasons as well. Indicators flag best practices that correlate with high achievement. Principal quality is also measured, and principals are being offered performance-based bonuses. Teacher bonuses are also in the works—although they are not tied to individual teacher effectiveness, but to the achievement of the school (the union won that one too).

In the mayor's previous career in the investment world, he created a three-screen display of data for stockbrokers. It brought together in one place more data than anyone else in the industry had ever assembled. It became known as the Bloomberg Screen, and quickly became an industry standard. The mayor would like the day to come when school principals have their own version of the Bloomberg Screen. Shouldn't principals know as much about the children in their care, as well as the teachers teaching them, as brokers know about stocks? Of course they should. And technology is making it possible.

Liberating Learning

A quarter century after *A Nation at Risk*, most observers believe the United States is still very much at risk.[51] Educational progress has fallen well short of expectations. But amid the disappointments are genuine reasons for hope. Through scientific research, we know much more about learning than we did twenty-five years ago. We also know much more about the qualities of successful schools. Most important, we know that learning can be strongly influenced by teaching and by schools. This may seem a strange thing to even acknowledge; isn't it obvious that schools impart knowledge that students wouldn't otherwise acquire? But it is equally clear that students learn a great deal from their families and communities, so much so that students from affluent and disadvantaged backgrounds generally achieve at vastly different levels. The achievement gap is so large that some question whether schools can ever overcome it. The evidence is now clear, though, that effective teaching and effective schools can help any student, regardless of background, to achieve at high levels.[52]

The evidence has emerged from numerous studies of student achievement, controlling for student background characteristics such as family income, family education, single-parent status, and the characteristics of student peers at school. Even with multiple disadvantages, students can achieve if they are subjected to the right teaching in the right schools. The easiest way to appreciate this fact is through the so-called "90/90/90" schools popularized by prominent education researcher Douglas Reeves.[53] Over the last decade many schools with 90 percent or more free- or reduced-price lunch students and 90 percent or more racial minority students have also managed to help 90 percent of their students achieve proficiency. All students can in fact achieve.

Research has also identified the factors most closely associated with student and school success. We have already dealt extensively with the influence of teachers. The effectiveness of the teacher is the number one influence on achievement—up to half a standard deviation in scientific terms, or enough to take a low-achieving student from failure to success in just a few years if taught by an effective teacher. We also know that effective teachers are not easily identified from their credentials, education, or experience (beyond the first few years of teaching). With the exception of verbal aptitude and subject matter competence, most of what makes a teacher successful is acquired on the job and can only be observed there.[54] Which is why great schools are those in which teachers receive intensive, ongoing professional development, are rigorously evaluated, and are retained or counseled out only after demonstrating the clear ability to help students learn.

Successful schools are also distinguished by their curricula. A good curriculum is broad, covering all of the subject areas. And it is demanding, taught to high standards. Too many schools water down their curricula to make them accessible to struggling students. Or they limit their curricula to the subjects for which they are being held accountable on tests—reading and math. But research now shows that reading comprehension is not adequately developed through skill drills; comprehension requires exposure to lots of rich text, with elevated vocabulary covering the gamut of the humanities and sciences.[55] Research also shows that students work up or down to expectations. Tracking kids into "appropriate" levels of course difficulty drives achievement downward for students in the lower tracks. One of the reasons inner-city Catholic schools succeed is that they cannot afford to offer tracks; everyone has to make it in an academically focused program.[56]

Another property seen time and again in successful schools is a distinctive culture. The best schools motivate their students to work hard, to believe in themselves, to understand that all students should aspire to attend college, and that success is within the reach of all students if they apply themselves with great diligence. The best schools have faculties focused on student achievement, taking ownership for results and holding themselves accountable. The best schools have relentlessly positive environments and can-do spirits, engaging every student in the life of the school and the pursuit of learning. Over the last decade, dozens of such schools have emerged under the guidance of national organizations such as the Knowledge Is Power Program (KIPP), Uncommon Schools, Achievement First, Green Dot, and Aspire. Each of these organizations has its own distinctive education program, but they share a culture of "no excuses" when it comes to student achievement.[57]

In light of all this, it is tempting to think that we as a nation now know what it takes for students to learn and for schools to succeed—we just need to do it! But this, of course, is far too easy. The keys to school success and student learning are qualities that the current system of public education militates against. Schools cannot rigorously evaluate teachers throughout their careers—certainly not using achievement data—to ensure that every teacher is high quality. Schools cannot build cultures of high expectations if they cannot ensure that every teacher on staff believes in it. Schools cannot teach broad and demanding curricula if they lack the teachers with the skills to help students meet these high standards. There are many reformers who say that all America needs to do is to carry out what we already know works—but they are being naive. They are ignoring the fundamental political obstacles that make these qualities of school success such a rarity.[58]

Technology is about to break down these political barriers. Improvements that have been nearly impossible will become much easier to bring about. And improvements that we cannot even anticipate will follow in their wake. Technology will make it much easier to differentiate instruction, as we have described. This innovation will enable students at vastly different achievement levels to master broad and demanding curricula—something even the best teachers struggle to bring about today. Technology will greatly improve teacher quality. By making teacher performance fully transparent, teachers will have a better chance of improving their practice, and administrators will be able to evaluate, develop, retain, and remove teachers based on actual merit. Fewer teachers will be necessary as students receive more instruction electronically. With fewer teachers to pay, teacher compensation can be improved, attracting stronger candidates into teaching and holding on to more of the top performers. Teachers will have more incentives to hone their craft, as their efficacy will be measured directly and their success will be rewarded. School cultures will also improve, as faculties will be less divided by the cynicism that grows from some teachers performing highly and others not carrying their weight—a well-documented problem in many public schools today. As schools become more efficient—changing the mix of teachers and technology and getting more bang (learning) for the buck—it is even possible that voters will look on schools more kindly, offering them more tax dollars to continue their upward course.

Technology is a frightening force to many educators, because it threatens to change the fundamentals of "their" system. But if we think of public education not as the current institution, but in terms of the vital responsibility it discharges—to ensure that every child receives a free, high-quality, effective education—then technology promises to be a very good thing. It will promote and accelerate the qualities that are now understood to drive learning. And it will make possible a world of learning that we are now only beginning to see. Students and teachers will soon inhabit virtual educational communities where they will interact regularly online, learning from one another in ways that have literally never before been possible. Teachers will have opportunities to teach in entirely new ways, opening up all sorts of creative and professional avenues not yet charted. Educators in other nations will play increasingly important roles in teaching American kids, and American teachers will spread their knowledge around the globe. Learning will be liberated from the physical and institutional constraints that now hold it back—and will be allowed to spread its wings.

5

THE RESISTANCE

The nation is on its way to a very different kind of education system. The speed of this transformation, however, is not going to parallel the dizzying pace of change in the economy. In that realm, new technologies are being put to creative use by countless entrepreneurs the world over who benefit from innovation and are aggressive in bringing their ideas, products, and services to market. With the incentives to innovate so strong, and with the power to innovate so decentralized, even the most traditional economies cannot help but be profoundly affected by the forces of disruption and rejuvenation that these technologies unleash.

Public education is run by the government. And because it is, innovation is only tangentially driven by economic or market forces. Whether innovation happens at all, and if so, what forms it takes and how extensive it is, are all determined in the political process: where the opportunities for blocking by powerful opponents are far greater, and the impediments to real progress are often insurmountable. In public education, innovations are not unleashed. They are resisted, fought, and crippled. Or at least they have been. But the times, we believe, are a-changing.

This chapter is about the politics of technology. We describe some of the early incursions of information technology into the protected realm of American public education—focusing mainly on the rise of virtual schools and the growth of data warehouses—and we show how they have been shaped by politics. As we do this, it is important to keep in mind that we are describing a moving target. These are just the beginning stages of innovation, and much of today's detail will soon be out of date. What matters are not the specific virtual schools, technologies, or data warehouses that currently exist, but the dynamism that spurs their emergence—and the structure of politics and power that tries to suffocate them and preserve the status quo. These are the fundamentals that are shaping the transformation of American education, and they are what need to be understood.

Technology and the Politics of Blocking

America's public schools are government agencies, and are typically granted monopolies (or close to it) over their own spheres of activity. Without much competition to worry about, they usually do not have to be innovative in order to receive their allotments of kids and money, and thus to survive. They are operated, moreover, by civil servants—administrators and teachers—whose pay and security are guaranteed whether they pursue innovation or not, and indeed, whether they perform well or not. Needless to say, monopoly and civil service go a long way toward snuffing out what we might call the internal incentives to innovate: the incentives of school personnel to adopt innovations on their own. They have little to gain from seriously pushing the envelope, as entrepreneurs do. And they have much to lose. For real technological innovation inevitably means changes in jobs, operating routines, organizational cultures, and much more—and these sorts of changes are threatening.[1]

Left to their own devices, then, the public schools are unlikely to be hotbeds of technological innovation. The schools themselves, however, are not the ultimate source of the problem—because they are not, after all, really left to their own devices. They are subordinates in a government hierarchy, subject to the authority of their elected superiors. And it is the elected superiors—especially those at the state and local levels: legislators, governors, school board members—who have shaped the American education system over the years, and who continue to make the key decisions about it. They are in charge. They determine whether the public schools join the information age. This being so, democratic politics is the natural transmission belt for bringing technology to public education. When innovations look promising, elected officials need to take concerted action within the policy process to assure that the public school system is open and responsive to change.[2]

It is wise not to expect too much from them, however. One reason is that, if public officials impose policies or rules that essentially order the schools to be innovative, these orders are likely to fail. The internal incentives to innovate are simply not there, and school personnel won't want to follow through. Plus, there is the problem of "asymmetric information": teachers and administrators know much more about the operation of schools than do elected officials—and they can use this advantage to circumvent top-down requirements, pursue innovation halfheartedly, and resist what they don't want to do. Elected officials might try to link funding to innovation, and thus make it rewarding; but here too school personnel can use their informational advantages and on-the-ground discretion to ensure that the innovations actually pursued are selectively chosen and nonthreatening.[3]

These problems are endemic to top-down managerial control. But if we assume the top-down system is here to stay (at least for a long while), then an obvious strategy for elected officials is to attack the information asymmetry. And technology makes it possible for them to do that. They can do it by collecting accurate, comprehensive information about the organization and performance of the public schools, compiling and storing the information in data warehouses—and using it to hold the schools accountable for boosting student achievement. This would give the schools greater incentives to innovate in whatever ways are productive at bringing about more achievement.

Another strategy—which can be implemented at the same time—is that public officials can authorize and encourage the creation of entirely new schools. These schools can then be staffed with believers and experts in the new technology: people who can be counted on to push for true innovation. Political scientists have long recognized that, if policy makers want to design new programs and have them succeed—think Franklin Roosevelt and the New Deal—they are well advised to create new agencies to carry those programs out, thus avoiding the entrenched interests and inbred cultures that tend to smother innovation in existing organizations. In this case, the new schools would promote innovation directly, because they would themselves be based on new technology. They would also promote innovation indirectly, because the regular public schools would have to compete with these new schools for kids and money—giving the existing system much stronger incentives to innovate, if only to keep what it already has.[4]

Elected officials have the authority to do these things anytime they want. They can create highly sophisticated data warehouses. They can fuel the growth of new high-tech schools. But the decisions they make are unavoidably political ones, fashioned within the policy process, and run smack into the buzz saw that has long plagued all aspects of American education reform: the politics of blocking. Teachers and administrators in the regular public schools know that if new types of high-tech schools were created, they would attract children and money away from their own schools—threatening their jobs, their security, and much of what they value in the educational status quo. They have every incentive to stop this from happening, and they are represented by powerful interest groups fully capable of taking political action on their behalf. Similarly, they know that the information contained in data warehouses will be used by their superiors in government to try to change and control their operations—and that it has the capacity, among other things, to identify poorly performing teachers and allow pay to be linked to teacher performance. So they have incentives to obstruct these developments as well.

It would be nice if elected officials could be counted on to resist this kind of defensive action by vested interests, and simply do what needs to be done for kids. But this is not the way politics works. Elected officials are responsive to power. And the exercise of political power by the teachers unions and other education groups has the effect of transmitting their own status-quo bias to elected officials, many of whom, out of fear for their own jobs, will use their authority to oppose, water down, or delay the introduction of new technology into the education system—and avoid creating new structures that promise major change.

The real problem, then, is the politics of blocking. Because of it, technological change is unlikely to come quickly or easily to the public schools. This is the baseline, the starting point from which any analysis must begin. In the discussion that follows, we will take a look at what has actually happened in the United States over the last decade or so, as the information age has offered up a cornucopia of opportunities for productive innovation. We will show that, for the most part, the system has embraced technology with cool reserve, adopting only those aspects that allow for safe, incremental change. We will also show that, when it comes to changes that are bigger and bolder, the opponents have used their political power to resist—and they have largely been successful, keeping the lid on what would otherwise have been an explosion of innovative activity.

There is more to the story, though. In technology, the powers that be are up against a monumental social force that is changing the world, and is truly historic in scope and magnitude. Social change is being thrust upon the education system from the outside, whether its protectors like it or not. The defenders of the status quo are trying to resist it, just as they have resisted all other threats to their interests over the years. But total insulation is impossible. The information revolution generates ideas about learning, about cost-effectiveness, about school management, about the transparency of performance, about the desirability of technological change. It generates entrepreneurs to pursue these ideas. It generates new and unanticipated opportunities to act. And it generates incentives to take advantage of these opportunities—even, as we will see, among state and district officials who are threatened by major change and want to make sure it doesn't happen.

For these reasons and more, the politics of blocking cannot entirely succeed. The defenders are at their most powerful right now, as technology begins its incursions into American public education. But there are already cracks in their retaining walls. And innovations are slowly seeping in and gaining a foothold.

Technology at the School Level

Let's begin by putting politics in the back seat for the moment and asking how teachers and administrators have adapted to the information age. They have few incentives to be break-the-mold innovators. But they don't perform their jobs in a vacuum either, and we shouldn't expect them to resist technology altogether.

The demands they get from students and parents are clearly protechnology. Students are high-tech natives these days. Their lives revolve around computers, the Internet, and the latest cutting-edge products—developments that they find exciting and richly rewarding. Parents want their kids to get the best education possible; and in the modern era, with computers at the forefront of social and economic change—and central to their kids' futures—it is only natural for them to want schools that are technologically up to speed.

The schools also get protechnology signals from their political superiors. This is not to say that, once power and vested interests are factored into the equation, public officials will push for major innovations. But rather that, because policy makers at all levels are responsible for the quality of the schools, and because they are electorally motivated to show they are doing something tangible to promote it, they tend to see technology as a progressive approach that makes good sense.

Teachers and administrators, then, are subject to expectations all around that they modernize their schools and keep up with the times. They also live in the same technologically oriented society that parents, students, and public officials do; and they recognize that computers can improve their work lives in a host of ways, from record keeping to course organization to student research to communication. The upshot is that they have good reasons to seek out technology on their own, and not to remain permanently stuck in the outdated pencil-and-paper mode of yesteryear. The problem, however, is that they only have incentives to make the most incremental of changes—changes that are helpful but don't threaten anyone's jobs or established routines. Their approach to technology is rooted in the status quo. It is about how to make the existing system work better without really changing it.

In a superficial sense, the public schools have come a long way during the last decade in embracing technology. We saw in the last chapter that schools have become universally connected to the Internet, as have most individual classrooms. But we also saw that the use of technology has hardly transformed teaching or learning. As recently as 2005, fully three-quarters of teachers reported that the students in their classrooms had to share or take turns using just a few available computers—a clear indication that computers are not central to in-school learning activities, or to teaching itself.[5] The reality is, the typical American classroom may have one or two computers with access to the Internet; and although most schools have computer labs, they cannot give all teachers continuous access, and they tend to be used by just a small portion of the faculty.[6]

Surveys of students highlight the stark incongruity between their high-tech lives on the outside—a world of cell phones, iPods, text-messaging, IM chatting, Internet searches, and all the rest—and the limited role of technology inside the schools. The common theme is one of frustration. Students complain that there are too few computers, too many limits on computer time and Internet use, and too little reliance on computers for class assignments and research—explained in part, they say, by excessive teacher and administrator concern about fairness (some kids may not have their own computers at home) and inappropriate behavior (access to pornography, for example). What they want is a technology-rich educational environment in which they have the freedom to roam and discover and interact. What they get, in their view, are limited computer and Internet resources, lots of restrictions, teachers who lack knowledge and interest in technology—and an approach to education that looks pretty much as it always did.[7]

Keen observers of public education tend to agree that computers have not had much impact thus far on the way most courses are actually taught, or on the way the public schools go about the business of educating children. Larry Cuban, who has been following the role of technology in the schools for many years and is perhaps the most widely cited scholar on the topic, argues that computers have been "oversold and underused" in public education: oversold because (in his view) they don't actually have that much to contribute, and underused because they conflict with the traditional culture and routines that have long governed how teachers go about their jobs. After a study of schools in California's Silicon Valley—where, one might presume, schools would be most likely to put technology to productive use—Cuban concludes that computers have barely made a dent in the traditional routines of American schooling:

> Teachers have been infrequent and limited users of the new technologies for classroom instruction. If anything, in the midst of the swift spread of computers and the Internet to all facets of American life, "e-learning" in public schools has turned out to be word processing and Internet searches. ... Teachers at all levels of schooling have used the new technology basically to continue what they have always done.[8]

Finally, we need to recognize (again) that state policy and funding decisions are relevant to what schools do as well. States have taken action in recent years, for instance, to provide more money to the schools for computer equipment, to require that teachers and administrators become better trained in technology, and to encourage schools to become more technologically advanced. To put it mildly, there is no evidence that these efforts have put the public school system at the cutting edge of educational innovation. But clearly, there are more computers in classrooms, more assignments and research involving the Internet, more teacher awareness of technology. Some progress has been made.[9]

These efforts are further advanced in some states than others. *Education Week* has been carrying out regular studies of how technology is put to use in the public schools, and in a recent report gave the states overall "technology grades," based on various indicators measuring "access to technology" (for example, students per instructional computer), "use of technology" (for example, whether students are tested on technology), and "capacity to use technology" (for example, whether state licensing requirements for teachers and administrators require technology course work or knowledge). For 2008, the numerical scores across the nation vary from a low of 60 (for the District of Columbia) to a high of 95 (for West Virginia).[10]

Doubtless many factors explain why some states seek out technology more than others, and we can't provide an in-depth analysis here. But the provocative thing about these technology grades is that the top scorers are almost all from southern and border states—where the teachers unions are the weakest. In Figure 5.1, we display the relationship visually by taking a general measure of union strength—the percentage of a state's teachers that belong to unions—and presenting the average technology score within groups of states. As the figure shows, the average technology score drops as union membership grows—from roughly 81 at lower levels of unionization to about 73 at higher levels of unionization.

The aspects of technology measured by *Education Week* hardly represent a challenge to the system. We would expect the unions to focus their political energies and have the greatest political impact on changes that are the most innovative and threatening. It is surely interesting, however, that even when it comes to changes that seem normal and manageable, at least by today's standards, technology appears to be advancing more quickly in states where the unions are weakest.

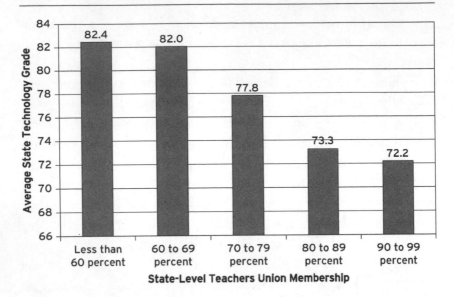

Figure 5.1 State Technology Grades, by Teachers Union Membership

Source: Source for data on technology grades: Editorial Projects in Education, "Technology Counts 2008."

Source: Source for data on union membership: National Center on Educational Statistics, *School and Staffing Survey 2003–04*.

Resistance to Cyberschools

Almost surely, if American education is going to take best advantage of true, cutting-edge innovation, progress calls for public officials to create—or somehow allow for the creation of—*new* schools that are operated by people committed to new technological approaches, particularly those that involve distance learning. But the big question is: can public officials really be counted on to do this?

In *Disrupting Class*, a recent book on technology and education that is attracting much attention, Clayton Christensen and his coauthors offer a provocative—and very positive—answer.[11] Their thinking is guided by Christensen's theory of "disruptive innovation," which was developed (in past books) to explain technological innovation in the private sector. The notion is that

the successful innovators tend to be new firms that target constituencies not being served by the established firms, and whose
new-wave products thus do not compete against—and do not
threaten or provoke the resistance of—the major players, who
themselves have strong incentives to continue doing what they
are doing. The new firms get a foothold in the market by moving
into these novel niches, and over time they (and other entrants
that jump on the bandwagon) are able to get established, develop
the quality and power of the technology, create a massive new
market—and the innovations take over, swamping the status quo.

Just such a dynamic was triggered by Apple, for example,
in introducing its personal computer in the late 1970s. It mar-
keted the personal computer as a toy for children, thus avoiding
direct competition with DEC and other established makers of
mainframe and minicomputers. For the consumers of mainframe
and minicomputers, the personal computer was not a substitute,
because it was not as good (even remotely) at performing the
functions they needed. Apple's market was people who were *not*
consumers of these products: people for whom the alternative to
a mainframe or minicomputer was simply nothing. By market-
ing to nonconsumers and by "competing against nothing," Apple
did not provoke the active opposition of the big boys. And as
the technology rapidly developed and other entrants joined the
fray, personal computers ultimately flourished and dominated the
market.

Christensen and his colleagues argue that technology will
triumph in public education in the same way that it has tri-
umphed in the private sector. Schools organized around distance
learning can offer AP physics or remedial math or Mandarin or
whatever local districts are not offering; and they can cater to
constituencies—students who are gifted, in need of specialized
courses, in rural or inner-city areas, in need of extra credits for
graduation, and so on—that are underserved by the current system. In so doing, these new schools can compete against nothing,
and district and state officials responsible for running the established public schools will not see them as threatening. Indeed,

public officials want to serve these constituencies if they can. And with budgets constrained and districts limited in the range of course work and teaching they can provide, the new virtual schools will be welcomed as a cost-efficient way of handling the more specialized educational needs that the districts can't otherwise handle. The work will essentially be outsourced to them—as contractors at the periphery of the system—with the districts retaining their core educational functions (at least at the beginning). These arrangements, beneficial to all concerned, thus allow virtual schools to move into the educational system, get a foothold, develop their technologies, and expand their markets. And very quickly—within ten years or so, the authors claim—virtual schooling will dominate and the education system will be transformed.

We agree that these forces will allow virtual schools to establish a presence in public education. It is true and enormously significant that virtual schools have much to offer underserved constituencies. It is also true and enormously significant that budget constraints, limited capacity, and constituency demand will give public officials persuasive reasons (in some cases) to turn to virtual schools as new, less costly providers of a wider array of services. These are key factors that do indeed allow virtual schools to seep into the system, and to serve as a catalyst for the transformation to come. But however important these factors are, they are not enough to explain the dynamics of educational continuity and change—because something about the logic is not quite right. Something fundamental is missing.

The problem is that public education is not part of the private sector, and its dynamics cannot be explained as though it is. Public education is *part of government*. New schools—and everything else about the education system—must be authorized within the political process, and powerful groups with a stake in the status quo can use their considerable power to block innovations they don't like. Blocking is vastly easier in the public sector than in the private sector. And the more "disruptive" the innovation, the more likely that it will be blocked. In addition, the new virtual schools are not really "competing against nothing" in public education, nor are the students they attract "nonconsumers." Aside from homeschoolers, the students who attend or take classes from virtual schools come from the regular public schools, and even if these students are seeking course work that isn't offered at all by the districts, the availability of virtual-school options allows children (or "parts" of children, depending on how many credits they take virtually) to leave the regular public schools, followed by money and jobs—and this strikes at the heart of union and district well-being. In the politics of education, then, the unions and the districts can hardly be expected to approach technology as a benign force with much to offer underserved constituencies. They will see it as a threat to their self-interest: one that needs to be limited, contained, and stripped of its dynamism.

Whether virtual schools ultimately triumph, therefore, is not just a story about innovation or underserved constituencies or budget constraints, although these elements—as we'll argue below—are all pivotal to the seeping-in stage of technological change. In the end, it is unavoidably a political story: a story of formidable power, a story of fierce resistance, a story of whether and how this resistance will eventually be overcome. Like Christensen and his colleagues, we are optimistic about the end result. The system will be transformed. But owing to the nature of politics, we see the process of change as much more difficult and conflictual—and taking much more time to come to fruition.

State-Level Virtual Schools

The unions and the school districts are threatened by technology, and have incentives to use the political process to resist. But what exactly will they do? What strategies will they follow? The fact is, their task is not so straightforward. They operate in a democratic system that is at least partially responsive to public opinion, and the world is changing around them. Technology is popular. And virtual schooling clearly has the potential to provide substantial benefits at very attractive costs to a variety of constituencies.

There are two implications; one political, the other practical. The political implication is that unions and school districts would have to be politically tone-deaf to stake out a public position that is diametrically opposed to all forms of virtual schooling. And if they did, even with all their power, a strategy of abject opposition might provoke a damaging backlash—for policy makers are *not* politically tone-deaf, and many want to take some sort of action that pleases the public and extends services to the underserved.

The practical implication is that the school districts themselves, along with education officials at the state level, actually have something to *gain* from outsourcing certain kinds of learning activities to virtual schools—because in a budget-constrained world, just as Christensen and colleagues have emphasized, the districts are much better able to satisfy the needs of students and parents (as well as the expectations of citizens generally) by taking advantage of the wide array of specialized services that virtual schools have to offer, and that the districts can't afford to provide on their own. Considerations of threat aside, then, districts and states have reason to see virtual schooling as beneficial—as long as it is designed to be supplementary to, and supportive of, the regular public schools.

The political and the practical dovetail nicely to yield a strategy of engagement that transcends the knee-jerk rejection of virtual schooling, and that allows the defenders of the system to take an open, even supportive approach to certain limited forms of distance learning and outsourcing. Their goal is not to block virtual schooling entirely, but to engineer a muted process of change that isn't unduly threatening. As a result, the political gates are partly open—and a good deal of seepage is occurring.

Today, the prime expression of this "acceptable" seepage takes the form of state-level virtual schools, which have recently been created by state governments to augment and support the traditional public school system—not to compete with it. Of all the forms that virtual schools might take, this one is the least threatening, and indeed offers (or appears to offer) the traditional system an opportunity to co-opt technology for its own sustenance. As these new state-level virtual schools have been adopted, there have been political issues raised—legitimately—about who will pay for them, how much they should cost, how they should be held accountable, and so on. But where they have been adopted, there have been no political battles to try to stop them.[12]

As of 2007–08, twenty-six states had set up state-level virtual schools, with one more (Texas) scheduled to begin operation in 2008–09.[13] The typical school is at the high school level (although sometimes middle school grades are included), and provides an array of courses that are unavailable to many students in their regular schools, including AP courses. The basic purpose of these schools, then, is to serve constituencies that are underserved by the regular schools. Funding aside, this is a good thing for the local districts, because it relieves them of the pressure of providing specialized courses that they cannot afford to provide, given their very real budget constraints. It is also a good thing for policy makers, who can get credit for providing additional educational services to constituencies that clearly need and want them.

Importantly, as far as defenders of the system are concerned, these virtual schools do not enroll the whole child. Students remain enrolled in their local districts and simply take a course or two from the state virtual school. When they do this, they are exercising choice—but the districts do not lose the students in the process, as typically happens with school choice programs. The virtual schools do not grant degrees. Students continue to get their degrees and take the bulk of their courses from their local districts. Politically this is crucial, for it greatly reduces the threat of having virtual schools participate in the system.

The threat is further reduced by the way these state-level virtual schools are funded. Approaches vary, but it is often the case that, when students take one or more classes from the state virtual school, the local district does not lose funding or is only charged a small fee. The state virtual schools usually get all or most of their money in lump sums from year to year: from annual legislative appropriations, department of education budgets, in-novation funds, and so on, depending on the state. Politically, lump-sum funding is a favorite arrangement because it does not take money from the regular public schools, and still allows the virtual schools to get established. By putting ceilings on school finances, moreover, it also limits how many teachers the virtual schools can hire, how much can be spent developing curricula, and the like, and thus how many students they can enroll—which limits their growth unless more money is forthcoming. This too minimizes the threat to the regular public schools.

As for how many students these schools currently enroll: it's not entirely clear. The problem is that, because they don't enroll whole students—the typical student appears to take one or two courses—there is no obvious way to calculate enrollment, and different schools often do it differently. We attempted to clarify matters by contacting schools directly and asking for information on one straightforward measure: the number of unique students participating in their programs during the 2007–08 school year. But not all schools were able to provide this information. When they weren't, we had to fall back on information—which many schools routinely provide—on their total enrollments in "half-credit" (semester-long) courses during 2007–08. This measure overcounts the number of unique students, because some students enroll in more than one course. But at least it does a reasonable job of conveying the size of their programs. Table 5.1 sets out these enrollment figures.

Although the data don't allow for easy comparisons across schools, one thing is abundantly clear: the Florida Virtual School is by far the largest, with an enrollment in 2007–08 of almost 100,000 unique students. It is in a league of its own. Indeed, it appears to have more students than all the other virtual schools combined. Most states have virtual schools with several thou-sand students or less—Colorado's program served 1,507 students in 2007–08, for instance, Wisconsin's served 1,100, and Illinois' served 3,200. Despite the high bar set by Florida, though, there are a few that seem to be moving ahead especially quickly. Alabama's ACCESS Distance Learning, for example, was just started in 2005, but already had 18,995 half-credit course registrations during 2007–08. And North Carolina's Virtual Public School, which began in 2007, had 17,626 course registrations during that first year of operation—a remarkable achievement.

There are roughly fifty million public school students in the United States. Even if it were possible to calculate the precise number of students enrolled (very part-time) in these state level online programs, the total would surely come to less than three-tenths of a percent of the public school student population: hardly much of a threat to the existing system. Most of the virtual enrollments, moreover, are due to the disproportionate size and success of the Florida Virtual School. Nonetheless, virtual schooling is expanding nationwide at a rapid clip. The number of states offering these programs has jumped from five in 1999 to the twenty-six offering them today; and many of their virtual schools have seen enrollments soar year after year—a measure of pent-up demand by underserved students and parents. To take but one example: the Utah Electronic High School has seen its enrollment jump from 3,124 students in 2004–05 to 6,763 in 2007–08, more than doubling its size in just three school years. For virtual schools all across the country, the best prediction for the immediate future is for continued rapid expansion.

The Florida program is likely to play a key role in this growth. It is not only large and well developed, but it is also a pioneer of the virtual school movement (started in 1997) and highly regarded on academic grounds—and for these reasons it is likely to serve as a model that encourages the diffusion of similar innovations across states. Research on American public policy has shown that historically this is the way policy innovations are often adopted, whether the substance is about welfare, the environment, health care, or education: first-adopters move into uncharted terrain to set up programs, the remaining states learn from their pioneering efforts, and the innovations spread based on successful models.[14]

Table 5.1 State-Level Virtual Schools

School	Start Year	Number of Students, 2007–08
ACCESS Distance Learning (Alabama)	2005	18,955*
Arkansas Virtual High School	2000	6,398*
Colorado Online Learning	1998	1,507
Connecticut Virtual Learning Center	2008	250*
Delaware Virtual School	2008	283*
Florida Virtual School	1997	97,132
Georgia Virtual School	2005	4,724
Hawaii E-School	1996	800
Idaho Digital Learning Academy	2002	6,619*
Illinois Virtual High School	2001	3,200
Innovative Digital Education and Learning New Mexico	2007	246*
Kentucky Virtual Schools	2000	2,214*
Louisiana Virtual School	2000	4,800
Maryland Virtual Learning Opportunities Program	2002	398
Michigan Virtual High School	2000	10,849*
Mississippi Virtual Public School	2006	5,025*
Missouri Virtual Instruction Program	2007	2,000
North Carolina Virtual Public School	2007	17,626*

North Dakota Center for Distance Education	1995	1,808*
South Carolina Virtual School Program	2006	7,389*
South Dakota Virtual High School	2007	740
Texas Virtual School Network	2009	N/A
University of Oklahoma High School	2000	580
Utah: The Electronic High School	1994	6,763
Virtual Virginia	2003	6,052*
West Virginia Virtual School	2000	1,367
Wisconsin Virtual School	2000	1,100
Nevada: Clark County School District Virtual High School**	1998	1,455
Tennessee State Virtual School (E4TN)**	2005	3,101*
Virtual High School (Massachusetts)**	1996	9,789

Notes: Methods of calculating enrollment and number of students vary across virtual schools. Unless otherwise indicated, the third column figures represent the number of unique students served by the state-level virtual school during the 2007–08 academic year.

*Number of half-credit (semester) enrollments; number of students not available.

**Not an actual state-level virtual school; school might be considered a "de facto" state-level virtual school due to the size or nature of the program.

Source: E-mail and phone correspondence with individual virtual schools; Southern Regional Education Board, *Report on State Virtual Schools,* August 2008; Evergreen Consulting Associates, "Keeping Pace with K–12 Online Learning," November 2008.

Another development that augers well for the future is that funding for the Florida Virtual School has recently been changed, so that it receives revenue on a per-student basis rather than through lump-sum appropriations. Now, when a student enrolls in a (one-credit) FLVS course, the school receives funding equal to one-sixth of what a school district normally receives from the state for a full-time student—and the "sending" district loses that amount.[15] With the new funding model, there are no limits on FLVS's future growth, because it receives payments for every student that it attracts, and is able to pay for additional teachers and other inputs as its enrollments grow. The artificial ceiling on its expansion has been eliminated. If other states follow Florida's lead on funding—and as programs increase in size, overall budget constraints make it the practical way to go—virtual programs are sure to expand dramatically.

Politically, as we said, these state-level virtual schools have not been very controversial thus far. But politics and power are hardly irrelevant. They are always lurking in the background, conditioning everything that happens. It is surely no coincidence that in Florida the governorship and both houses of the legislature have been controlled by Republicans during this entire period, and the teachers unions have been politically weaker than in many other states, especially with their Democratic allies out of power.

If we look across all states, in fact, there is evidence that this relationship between state-level virtual schools and the political environment obtains more generally. Consider, for instance, the simple comparisons in Figure 5.2, in which states are grouped according to the percentage of their teachers who are unionized. As the figure shows, the percentage of states with state-level virtual schools drops steadily as the unionization of teachers grows—from a high of 100 percent in the least unionized states to a low of 35 percent in the most unionized states. So although these state-level virtual schools have emerged without major political fights, the apparent lack of controversy may be somewhat misleading. It is likely that in the states where they have not emerged—many of them states with strong unions—serious

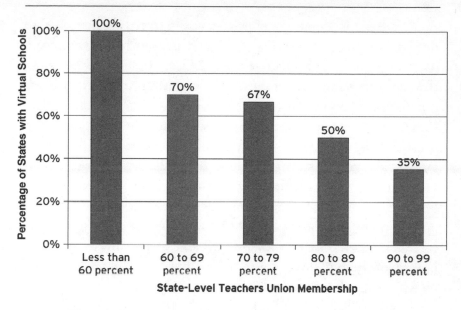

Figure 5.2 State Virtual Schools, by Teachers Union Membership

Source: Source of data on state virtual schools: Evergreen Consulting Associates, "Keeping Pace with Online Learning."

Source: Source of data on teachers union membership: National Center on Educational Statistics, *School and Staffing Survey 2003–04*.

proposals have simply been kept off the table and not allowed to become the focus of political attention and conflict.

As far as the future is concerned, the unions and the school districts almost surely see dark clouds on the horizon. For now, the kinds of small supplementary programs that many states have developed are just fine, even good, because they augment the system's own services and make their constituencies happier. But they do not want these programs to get out of hand, to the point where they are competing with the districts for funds or getting so large that many courses that could be taught locally are instead being taught at a distance. Yet this is exactly what is likely to happen.

Within states that already *have* such programs, demand is likely to grow by leaps and bounds over time as underserved constituencies increasingly find out about the options available to them and more people participate. The districts are even likely to be complicit in this growth—because the supplementary nature of the programs is helpful to them in the short term, allowing them to offload services that they can't provide with their own dollars and still see that constituencies are taken care of. Within states that do *not* have such programs, on the other hand, another dynamic is likely to be at work. The Florida model is likely to loom large—for even in strong-union states, underserved constituencies will see what their counterparts in the first-adopter states are getting, and they will begin demanding the same. Once technology makes these kinds of schools possible, and once certain states have demonstrated that they are workable on a grand scale, policy makers in the remaining states will be hard pressed to deny their own citizens what others already have.

In future years, as all of this picks up steam and as state-level virtual schools grow and spread, there is more likely to be overt political conflict. The defenders will become more and more alarmed, and they will increasingly need to go public with their opposition. But for now, the camel's nose is well inside the tent.

Cyber Charters

For now, the state-level virtual schools represent a seepage of technology into the public school system that is acceptable to the powers that be. But there is also significant seepage from another source entirely, one that is not acceptable at all to the unions and (most) school districts: a new and growing population of cyber charters—charter schools that enroll students on a full-time basis, provide them with full curricula via distance learning, grant degrees, and actively compete with the regular public schools for students and funds.

The unions and school districts find cyber charters quite threatening. The most compelling concerns, by orders of magnitude, have to do with jobs and money. By their nature, cyber charters can attract students from anywhere in the state, and thus can affect many districts at the same time. They are not, moreover, just getting a small fraction of a student, as the state-level virtual schools do, but the entire student—so the impact per student is much greater. Parents also tend to play a big role in these schools, for students often do their work from home, and the schools rely on parents to monitor their kids and facilitate the learning process—and thus to do things that certified teachers do, and are paid for, in the regular public schools. Parents, in other words, are "taking" teachers' jobs, and making it possible for cyberschools to have an even lower ratio of teachers to students than they otherwise could.

Other issues deepen the opposition. One is that cyberschools sometimes contract with private, for-profit companies—the most prominent of which are K12 and Connections Academy—to provide curricula and related services, and the unions and districts are almost always opposed to for-profit companies playing a role in public education. They want public dollars to be spent on public agencies staffed by unionized public workers. Another issue arises because cyber charters attract large numbers of students who were previously being homeschooled. The basis for the attraction is obvious: students can remain at home, yet they benefit from certified teachers, a structured curriculum, and other components of a "real" school. Because they were not previously on the books as public school students, however, the government was not paying for their education, and their enrollment in cyberschools means that new money has to be found—which, if taken from the education budget, leaves less money for the regular public schools.

The battle lines are starkly drawn: the unions and (most) districts would like to prevent these schools from emerging. The main problem they face is that in many states, entrepreneurs who want to set up cyberschools do not have to go through the legislature to do it. They can use their states' charter laws instead: laws that, whether by authorization or omission, give them many opportunities for setting up new cyberschools, and make their efforts much more difficult to block.

Forty states now have legal frameworks that allow for the creation of charter schools: public schools operated largely independently of the districts. These laws allow certain public actors—districts and possibly other entities, such as universities or state boards—to authorize charters, and they set out the rules under which the schools are operated and funded. Charter laws have been around for some time, many since the early to mid-1990s, and were designed before the technologies for cyber charters were well developed and before they were seen by defenders of the system as any kind of practical threat. They were barely on anyone's radar screens. For these reasons, and because amending charter laws is often contentious and difficult, many of today's state charter laws do not deal with cyber charters at all. In twenty states, the law explicitly allows charter schools to be set up as virtual schools. In many other states with charter frameworks, cybers are neither allowed nor disallowed—yielding a gray area of legal ambiguity that gives entrepreneurs the opportunity to act. As they see it, they are setting up charters and following the rules of the law, and nothing in the law says they can't create virtual schools.[16]

Because of charter laws, then, the power to authorize and establish cyberschools is decentralized into many hands—and much more difficult to stop than a simple piece of legislation. There is more going on, and it is happening in many different places at once. As a result, the politics of cyber charters has a rather chaotic quality to it. The unions and districts have essentially been playing Whac-A-Mole, dealing with troublesome cyber situations as they arise—but turning around to find more and more popping up around them.

Despite these blocking attempts, cyber charters—aided by the flexibility of state charter laws—have been growing at a fast clip. Enrollments have tripled in the last two years, and the number of schools has doubled. As of 2007–08, there were 190 cyber charters nationwide, enrolling somewhere in the neighborhood of one hundred thousand students (see Table 5.2). Cyberschools were

Table 5.2 Virtual Charter Schools

State	Number of Virtual Charters	Total Enrollment	Year First Virtual Charter Opened
AK	1	325	1997
AR	2	496	2003
AZ	16	11,695	1995
CA	32	11,308	1993
CO	6	6,178	2001
FL	2	541	2002
GA	2	3,144	2004
HI	3	1,209	2000
ID	5	3,826	2001
IL	1	600	2006
IN	1	*	2008
KS	8	1,051	2001
MI	6	1,507	1995
MN	7	2,660	1996
NH	1	450	2008
NM	5	1,411	2000
NV	4	2,073	1999
OH	48	29,965	2000
OR	5	2,044	2000
PA	12	13,996	1998
SC	2	*	2008
TX	1	550	2006
UT	1	*	2008
WI	18	4,139	1999
WY	1	46	2004
Total	190	99,214	

*Schools are scheduled to open in 2008–09. A charter school qualifies as a virtual school if more than half of its curriculum is online.

Source: The Center for Education Reform.

present in only twenty-five of the forty states that have charter laws, however, and their distribution is quite uneven: while almost all states with cyber charters had between one and eight schools, Ohio had forty-eight, California had thirty-two, and Arizona and Wisconsin had eighteen and sixteen, respectively.[17]

Ohio is the obvious outlier here, and what has happened in that state is quite interesting. Put simply, a small number of cyber charters—which received their charters not from districts, but from higher-level authorizers—got organized and began attracting students statewide. Thousands of them. And the school districts, worried about losing money and enrollment, responded to the competition by setting up their own cyber charters: schools under their own control, designed to cater to the online needs of children within their geographic boundaries. They were enticed to go the charter route, rather than setting up regular public schools with online capabilities, because they could qualify for boatloads of federal funding that way—$450,000 per school.[18]

A closer look at the Ohio data shows that the vast majority of that state's cyber charters—thirty-seven of forty-eight—are actually set up by districts for their own children and typically have enrollments that are quite small. Most have less than a hundred students, many less than fifty. Thus, the outsized number of cyberschools for the state of Ohio, compared to other states, is somewhat misleading. The more meaningful figures are those for enrollment. By far the largest cyber charters in Ohio are the statewide charters run by for-profit and nonprofit organizations outside of district control. The largest of these is the Electronic Classroom of Tomorrow, with a 2007–08 enrollment of 7,323. Together, these statewide schools enroll more than 85 percent of the state's roughly thirty thousand cyber charter students—and this is where the competitive dynamic really comes from. A handful of cyber charters is accounting for most of it. Even so, the response of the school districts is a fascinating phenomenon in itself—a demonstration of what competition can do—and it contributes to the continued growth in online enrollments.[19]

As the Ohio case illustrates, the districts are not one-dimensional actors in the evolving world of virtual schooling. Throughout this chapter, we have emphasized that the districts have reason to view these schools as threats that siphon away students and money, and that they have incentives to fight back politically to prevent such schools from emerging and spreading. But this is not the only way they can respond. They may decide to fight back by setting up their own virtual schools, as they have in Ohio, seeing this as a way to please their local constituency and keep the students and money at home. And as we will see in the cases to follow, some districts—they are rare, but they are out there—may decide to do much more: by becoming aggressively entrepreneurial, and setting up virtual schools that actually take students and money away from other districts.

The unions, meantime, *are* pretty much one-dimensional. Even if they wanted to, they could not authorize charter schools on their own account. And there is little reason for them to support charters run by districts or other public organizations. Most charters are nonunion, operate outside of district collective bargaining agreements, and contribute to a weakening of union power. They take students and money from the regular public schools, which are unionized. Also, the local unions are bound together into powerful state federations, and their state-level leadership does not want its locals supporting innovations—such as virtual charters—that would lead them to compete with one another for students and money. There would be losers as well as winners, and plenty of discord. Districts can sometimes be surprising in their approach to virtual charter schools. The unions are more predictable.

The Politics of Cyber Charters

In this section, we take a closer look at what has happened in particular states as virtual charters have made their entrance and attempted to get established. These accounts suggest just how turbulent their early lives have been, and shed additional light on the roles that unions and districts have played in reacting to educational change.

Wisconsin provides a nice illustration. It has a charter law that allows districts to authorize charters, but until recently the law said nothing about whether the charters could be virtual schools. Wisconsin also has an open enrollment law, designed to give students more choice options, that allows charters to enroll students across district lines. As new technologies emerged, these laws created obvious openings for entrepreneurs to set up cyber charters—and for renegade districts that might be bold enough to try to increase their enrollments and revenues by attracting students from other districts.

This is exactly what the Appleton and Northern Ozaukee school districts had in mind, prompting them to become pioneers in virtual schooling. In the fall of 2002, the Appleton district set up the state's first virtual charter school, Wisconsin Connections Academy, as a joint venture with Connections Academy, a for-profit company. The district authorized and ran the charter school, and Connections provided the curriculum, the technology, the training, and other key components of its educational organization. In the fall of 2003, the Northern Ozaukee school district contracted with K12, another for-profit company, to form its own cyber charter called Wisconsin Virtual Academy.[20]

For both districts, the idea worked well. They attracted hundreds of new students, almost all of them from outside their own boundaries, and brought in more than $5,000 in new money for each of the new students. Proportionately, these funds represented a big change in district finances. In Northern Ozaukee, for example, the cyberschool's enrollment in the 2006–07 school year was 753—compared to 850 students enrolled in all of the district's regular public schools.[21] Thus, the district had "virtually" doubled in size. In both districts, most of the new money went to pay the costs of the cyberschools. But there was money left over, which the districts used to augment their other educational programs.

This is what innovation is all about: a new form of education was provided, students and parents were voluntarily choosing this new form in preference to the old, and the innovators—the school districts and their private partners—were benefiting from taking risks, making investments, and providing services that people value. But for the teachers unions (and for many affected districts), innovation was a threat that needed to be stamped out. Appleton and Northern Ozaukee were taking students and money from other districts, and this kind of cross-district competition was unacceptable. Worse, the virtual charters were joint ventures with for-profit companies, which the unions wanted to eliminate from public education.

So the unions went to court, filing lawsuits intended to put both these virtual charter schools out of business. Their strategy was to ensnare them in the rules of the traditional system: rules that were not designed with cyberschools in mind and could now be used as weapons. The suit against Appleton was filed in circuit court in September 2002, just as the school was first opening. It alleged that, under the charter school law, children are required to be physically present in the charter school they transfer to, which rules out virtual schools. It also argued that, under the open enrollment law, funding is based on the costs of traditional public schools, and the amounts transferred to virtual schools, which don't have the same costs, are thus excessive.

The judge ruled against the union on both counts in 2003, dismissing the case. The union then appealed. Shortly thereafter, in January 2004, the union filed a separate case against the Northern Ozaukee district, making the same arguments, but adding a new one: that parents were playing too large an instructional role and substituting for credentialed teachers—another violation of traditional rules. In March 2006, the union lost this case too, on all three grounds. It then appealed. At about the same time, the legislature managed to pass a bill that explicitly allowed for virtual schools, and set out new legal rules for their operation, in an effort to avoid these kinds of lawsuits. This was a major step forward. But the bill—opposed by the union—was then vetoed by the state's Democratic governor, Jim Doyle, whose election the union had supported.

The court cases slogged on. The union eventually dropped the Appleton appeal, and embraced the Northern Ozaukee case as its prime legal vehicle. Its efforts led in December 2007 to an appeals court decision that reversed the lower court and *favored the teachers unions on all counts*. The state was ordered to stop funding Wisconsin Virtual Academy for its out-of-district students (the vast majority of its total enrollment), and all virtual schools in the state were thereby placed in legal jeopardy.

Welcome to the politics of blocking. In a separation of powers system, there are many veto points, and the unions are pleased to seek vetoes wherever they can, and to keep trying until something finally works. Here the union lost in the lower courts but won at the appeals level—and blocked. It lost when a bill emerged from the legislature, but the bill was blocked before passing into law because the governor—their ally—vetoed it.

Politics never stops, though, and the union can never rest. Its appeals court victory sent shock waves through the charter school community, and the legislature quickly swung into action to see that the state's twelve cyberschools would not be shut down. After intense bipartisan negotiations, a bill emerged that recognized cyberschools in the law, allowed for their funding, imposed requirements for teacher certification and training, and required a state audit of costs and operations. Along the way, the governor "had thrown the bill into jeopardy by demanding a cap on enrollment for online schools—something the state teachers union desperately wanted."[22] He threatened a veto. And he got the cap, which limits the state's charter schools to an aggregate total of 5,250 students (compared to 3,400 at the time of the legislation). Unable to eliminate the cybers entirely, this became the union's main goal: to keep a tight lid on their enrollment. And it was achieved, in a big victory for the union. As time goes on, however, there will inevitably be greater and greater pressures to lift the cap—so the union cannot rest on its laurels. And it won't. It will keep trying to block.

In Pennsylvania, the main antagonist has been the Pennsylvania State School Boards Association (PSBA)—a representative of district interests, acting in alliance with the state teachers union—and the focus has been less on individual schools than on cyberschools generally. But the controversy there has otherwise been much the same. In 2001, as the number of cyber charters jumped from two to seven, and as the larger ones—the Pennsylvania Virtual Charter School and the Pennsylvania Cyber Charter School (introduced in the last chapter)—were in the process of attracting thousands of new students across district boundaries, "sending" districts found themselves being required to transfer their education dollars to the new cyber charters. The districts were up in arms about this, with hundreds of them refusing to pay—to the tune of many millions of dollars—and the state department of education threatened to withhold their education budgets unless they followed through. The PSBA, in support of the districts, went to court. It argued that cyber charters are not legal and that districts should not have to pay, pointing out that many of the students attending cyber charters were previously homeschooled, and claiming that homeschoolers were not covered by the state's charter law. A judge quickly ruled against the PSBA—which continued its fight in the legislature with help from the state teachers union.[23]

Shortly thereafter, a new law was passed transferring the authority over cyberschools to the state, adding new rules and regulations, and reimbursing districts for 30 percent of the costs when they lose students to these schools. Although the reimbursement was welcomed by the districts, the legislation was not anticyber—in part because both the legislature and the governorship were in Republican hands. Cyber charters remained legitimate, they continued to receive the same funding, and no limitations were placed on their growth. But this was hardly the end of it. The PSBA and the union have pushed on with the legislative fight and tried to get a bill through the state legislature—authored by a legislator who happens to be a former president of the PSBA—that would cut cyberschool funding by roughly half and subject them to more restrictive auditing and budgeting requirements.[24] In the meantime, many districts are still delaying or withholding their payments to cyber charters. The politics of opposition never stops.

Chicago provides another good example. The schools in that city came under mayoral control in 1995 after their rock-bottom performance spurred demands for change. An important part of the mayor's response was the Renaissance 2010 plan to replace sixty underperforming schools with more than a hundred smaller schools—which were to be operated under contract, or by outside providers, and would have more freedom and flexibility. One of these new schools, reformers hoped, would be the Virtual Charter School, a joint venture between the district and the for-profit company K12. The idea was that this virtual school could provide an entirely new kind of educational opportunity for up to six hundred students in the district.[25]

The Chicago Teachers Union (CTU) was vehemently opposed, and launched a political campaign to prevent the school from coming into existence. District officials (under mayoral leadership) weathered the storm and went ahead to approve the school's charter in January 2006; and in August, after a "tense and dramatic meeting," the state board of education voted 5–4 to authorize the plans to move ahead. The union was not about to give up, however, vowing it would "take swift and appropriate action to stop or block the opening of this school."[26] True to its word, the CTU filed a lawsuit in October challenging the school's right to exist. It argued that the school is "home-based," and thereby violates the state's charter school law. It also argued that under state law a school can only receive state funding if it provides "direct supervision" by certified teachers, which a virtual charter does not do.[27] For good measure, one of the union's Democratic allies in the state legislature then introduced a bill that would ban funding for charter schools engaged in virtual learning of any kind, and would prohibit the state board of education and local school boards from "establishing, maintaining, or in any way supporting any virtual schools or virtual classes for elementary or secondary students" in Illinois. So the Chicago Virtual Charter School is up and running—but its enemies are still out to get it, and indeed, they are looking for ways to prevent any similar schools from emerging anywhere in the state.

The best way to prevent virtual schools from emerging is through legislative action, assuming the opponents have enough power to make it happen. The courts, which played a prominent role in all of the above examples, are obviously very useful blocking tools, because it is relatively easy for the unions or the districts to simply file a lawsuit. Some judge at some level may agree with them. But the courts are interpreting statutes written by the legislature, which acts first and sets the framework for everyone else's actions. So the defenders' first preference, if and when they are capable of it, is to shape the statutes themselves. Also, the legislature is the source of public funds and the authority for their disbursement. These funding decisions, too, offer myriad opportunities for influence.

Not surprisingly, then, some of the most interesting and consequential attempts to undermine virtual schools have involved legislative action. Consider what happened recently in Indiana. Here the initiative for virtual schools came from Ball State University, which had already chartered nineteen schools in the state, and in early 2007 was moving ahead with the sponsorship of two cyber charters: Indiana Connections Academy and Indiana Virtual Charter School—the former in partnership with Connections Academy, the latter in partnership with K12. Both were scheduled to open in the fall, enrolling students statewide, with a total expected enrollment of over twenty-two hundred, and even more on waiting lists.[28]

But the necessary $21 million in funding had to come from the legislature, and the Indiana State Teachers

Association—variously arguing that the programs drain money from the public schools, that they spend precious public dollars on homeschoolers, that the true costs of virtual schooling are unknown, and that the programs are unproven—launched a high-profile lobbying campaign to stop these cyber charters in their tracks. After a fierce battle, the Republican-controlled Senate approved a budget for the virtual schools, but the Democratic-controlled General Assembly voted it down, leading to legislation on the final day of the 2007 legislative session that not only denied the schools funding, but placed a two-year moratorium on funding for *any* virtual schools—supposedly for the purpose of giving the state extra time to study their pros and cons.

Oregon is another case in point. In 2005 the Scio school district entered into a partnership with Connections Academy to create the Oregon Connections Academy, which aimed to enroll students statewide. Within months, the Oregon Education Association and its allies in the legislature were able to pass a bill requiring that any virtual school must enroll at least 50 percent of its students from the district in which it is based—thus putting a strict cap on their ability to recruit students outside district boundaries, and making it impossible for them to grow and develop. As a spokesman for Oregon Connections Academy noted at the time, quite correctly, "The whole idea of an online public school is that people would be able to attend from great distances. The 50 percent rule is a poison pill designed to kill that innovation."[29] So far, the state department of education has treated Oregon Connections Academy as being protected from this restriction, because its charter was signed before the legislation was passed. But the legislation applies to all virtual charters created after the legislation. And it will apply to Oregon Connections Academy too, once its current charter runs out and must be renewed. The lid is on.[30]

It is also on in California. Cyberschools there have had the misfortune of getting caught up in political controversies that, almost as soon as the state's 1992 charter law first took effect, have surrounded homeschool charters—which are not cyber charters, but schools that provide various sorts of educational services (books, curricula, teacher monitoring, and the like) to home-schooled children and their parents. As these schools proliferated, reports of profiteering and accounting irregularities set off waves of legislative activity—eagerly supported by the unions and their allies—to impose stricter regulations on these schools, if not elim-inate them entirely (which was seriously discussed). These battles went on for a decade. During this time, virtual schools were in their infancy and were not much of a threat—but the opponents didn't overlook them. Although they publicly highlighted the dangers of homeschool charters, their regulatory focus was on all "nonclassroom-based" forms of schooling—which included cyber charters. Thus, as the political battles over homeschooling led to restrictive legislation—in 1995 (SB399), 1998 (AB544), 1999 (SB434), and 2001 (SB740, whose details were filled in by subse-quent state school board rules)—the restrictions applied to cyber charters too, and these schools were heavily encumbered.[31]

Among other things, California's rules (a) allow a cyber char-ter to draw students from the county in which it is based, plus contiguous counties, but from nowhere else in the state; (b) give them full funding only if they spend 50 percent of their public funds on teacher salaries; and (c) require a student-teacher ratio no larger than that of the largest unified school district in its county. The rules, in other words, go a long way toward elim-inating the very features that are distinctive and advantageous about cyberschools, and force them to operate under geographic and staffing constraints that make them more like traditional schools. Much of the wind has been taken out of their sails—and it shows. As of 2007–08, there are only thirty-two cyber char-ters in the entire state. Most have enrollments of less than 500, and together they enroll just under 11,300 students: a drop in the bucket for a state with more than six million kids in the public schools.[32]

As these examples from all across the country help illustrate, the politics of blocking is ubiquitous. Wherever there are cyber charters or the potential for cyber charters, the unions and their allies are on the lookout for ways to block them. And they are quite successful. The flip side, however, is that they are up against a raging social force—the rise of technology—that is perpetually generating vast numbers and types of entrepreneurial efforts that they must try to stop. Their game plan is to block, and they are good at it, but they can't—and haven't—stopped them all. Despite the defenders' power, there *are* cyber charters, and they *are* growing and spreading. We have to remember that cyber charters are now in their most difficult period—the period of formation—in which the challenges of organization are greatest and the power of the defenders is at its height. Even under these conditions, they are making progress. It is slower progress than supporters might like, by a good bit. But it is progress nonetheless, and a key way that technology seeps into the system—creating a basis for the much bigger changes yet to come.

The Politics of Information

Technology does more than generate new schools. It also generates a sophisticated capacity to collect, store, and analyze *information*—and this too is an important and hugely consequential means by which technology is seeping into the system.

Abstractly, of course, information is what the technological revolution is all about. It is an information revolution. And for education in particular, as we discussed in Chapter Four, technology brings with it a dramatically enhanced ability to collect data on students, schools, teachers, finances, and other aspects of the education system, to store and manage all this information in computerized data warehouses—maintained by the states, most important, for the management of their schools—and to carry out analysis in concerted efforts to make schools more effective at promoting student achievement.

To most people, this probably sounds very boring. But to the teachers unions, it is not boring at all. It is threatening. Consider what has already happened, due to the advance of state-level accountability systems and No Child Left Behind. Frequent testing of students and grading of schools has generated substantial data about school performance, and these data are not only used by states to put pressure on low-performing schools to improve, but are also typically made public—which affects public opinion and gives rise to demands for change. Information on performance, in other words, translates into trouble for those who work in the schools: more pressure, more controls, more unwanted publicity. Their lives were much easier in the more serene days before accountability, when performance wasn't measured and no one really knew what was going on.

Technology compounds their problems. The broad reason is that it simply provides more and better performance information, which in turn spells more pressure, controls, and publicity. From the standpoint of unions and teachers, however—and they are the heavy hitters, politically—the most worrisome part of the information revolution is that modern data systems have the capacity to connect students to teachers and classrooms—and thus to provide objective data on the *performance of teachers*. With a well-constructed data warehouse, then, decision makers can know how much the students in each class are learning, and thus how well each teacher is doing his or her job. Care would have to be taken, of course, to make sure that the measures (test scores) are appropriate and fair. On that, everyone can agree. But well-formulated measures would inevitably show that some teachers are much better than others, and some are very bad. And once such information becomes available and known, it would be much more difficult for policy makers to embrace the myth that somehow all teachers are the same, that they all (even the bad ones) have a right to stay in the classroom, and that they should all be paid equally—principles that are at the core of union policy, and indeed basic to their solidarity and organization. The unions, therefore, have much to fear from good data. Especially data on teachers.

Which brings us, once again, to the politics of blocking. The unions have reason to want to prevent the states from building comprehensive data systems. But in this case, blocking is not so easy. First, they are in the awkward position of having to explain to policy makers why an objective, comprehensive database on the schools—including data on teachers, who are obviously the keys to learning—is somehow a bad thing. Good information is bad? This is a tough sell. Second, No Child Left Behind's regular testing and pressures for improvement have driven districts and states to begin amassing data anyway, as part of the new accountability regime; and in recent years the U.S. Department of Education has been giving out grants to state governments to create new data systems. Having failed to block No Child Left Behind, the unions are now caught in its backdraft.

Given the situation, the unions' best political strategy is to accept the reality and continued development of these data systems, including the collection of basic data on teachers. As with accountability, they can claim to "support" modern data systems—and avoid looking like Neanderthals in what would likely be a losing cause. They can then direct their fight more narrowly against those aspects of the information movement that are most threatening: the efforts to *link* teacher data to student data, and to *use* those data to measure the performance of teachers, evaluate them, determine their pay, or remove poor performers from the classroom.

This is basically how the unions have calibrated their strategy since the information revolution put data systems on the political map. For the most part, these systems are state-level issues. But during 2007, they became a national-level issue when No Child Left Behind was up for reauthorization. A bipartisan draft of the bill included a provision that required states to develop data systems containing "a unique statewide teacher identifier that remains consistent over time and matches all student records…to the appropriate teacher."[33] Remember, this was a bipartisan draft, supported by key Democrats as well as many Republicans, and the fact that it called for the linkage of student and teacher data speaks to the powerful appeal that comprehensive data systems have for policy makers in general. But the unions view the value of data very differently. And the National Education Association, which strongly opposed this provision, issued the following statement that nicely clarifies where the union stands:

> This language ... shreds all the safeguards that some states fought for in an effort to ensure that any statewide teacher database was separate and apart from any student database. This would require the linking of those databases into a single system.... The use of the data should be limited by statute to identifying teachers for additional professional development and for the use by individual teachers to improve instructional practices. There must be a limitation that the teacher data may not be used for evaluating teachers or determining their compensation.[34]

Movement toward comprehensive data systems is taking place all across the country, but the content and pace of their efforts varies from state to state. As of 2007, among the fifty states plus the District of Columbia (to simplify, we will henceforth treat D.C. as a state), forty-five have developed data systems that contain unique statewide identifiers for all their students, making it possible to "follow" each student from year to year across any schools he or she may attend. This in itself is a major achievement. In forty-nine states, these data systems contain information on student demographics and program participation; forty-six states have the capacity to measure academic growth by matching student test scores from year to year; forty-nine states collect student-level data on graduation and dropping out; and the more sophisticated state systems contain many more kinds of data as well.

One type of data in particular is relatively rare at this point: only eighteen states have unique teacher identifiers that allow for a linking of teacher and student data.[35] Table 5.3 sets out the states that do and do not have data systems with teacher identifiers. What immediately stands out is that most of these states are southern or border states—states that are relatively conservative,

Table 5.3 Teacher Identifiers

State	Teacher Identifier?	State	Teacher Identifier?
Alabama	Yes	Indiana	No
Arkansas	Yes	Iowa	No
Delaware	Yes	Kansas	No
Florida	Yes	Maine	No
Georgia	Yes	Maryland	No
Hawaii	Yes	Massachusetts	No
Kentucky	Yes	Michigan	No
Louisiana	Yes	Minnesota	No
Mississippi	Yes	Missouri	No
New Mexico	Yes	Montana	No
Ohio	Yes	Nebraska	No
Pennsylvania	Yes	Nevada	No
Rhode Island	Yes	New Hampshire	No
South Carolina	Yes	New Jersey	No
Tennessee	Yes	New York	No
Utah	Yes	North Carolina	No
West Virginia	Yes	North Dakota	No
Wyoming	Yes	Oklahoma	No
Alaska	No	Oregon	No
Arizona	No	South Dakota	No
California	No	Texas	No
Colorado	No	Vermont	No
Connecticut	No	Virginia	No
District of Columbia	No	Washington	No
Idaho	No	Wisconsin	No
Illinois	No		

Source: Data Quality Campaign, 2007 NCEA State P–12 Data Collection Survey Results: State of the Nation.

with relatively weak teachers unions. In Figure 5.3 we again break the states down into groups according to the unionization of their teachers, and look at the percentage of states in each group that have data systems with the capacity to link students and

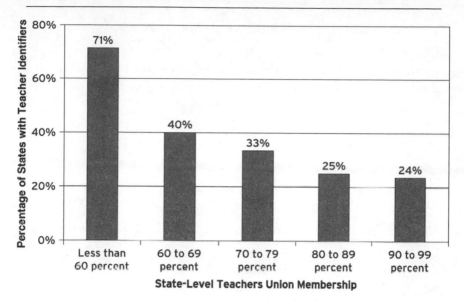

Figure 5.3 States with Teacher Identifiers, by Teachers Union Membership

Source: Source of data on teacher identifiers: Data Quality Campaign, *2007 NCEA State P–12 Data Collection Survey Results: State of the Nation.*

Source: Source of data on teachers union membership: National Center on Educational Statistics, *School and Staffing Survey 2003–04.*

teachers. What we find is that 71 percent of the least unionized states have this crucial data component, and that the percentage declines steadily until it reaches a low of 24 percent among the most unionized states. This is the same basic pattern as for virtual schools—which is telling, as virtual schools and teacher identifiers have little to do with one another aside from their impact on union interests. To get a better sense of how the unions approach data issues, let's take a look at a few specific cases.

The Data Quality Campaign keeps track of the states' progress in improving their data systems, focusing on ten key dimensions. One of the top-scoring states is Texas, which systematically collects and stores data on nine of the ten dimensions. There is one dimension on which it falls short: it lacks unique teacher identifiers that link to student data. In fact, Texas has included teacher identifiers in its data system since the 1986–87 school year—but they do not link to student data. During 2007, however, there was a serious effort within the Republican-controlled Texas legislature, supported by state business leaders, to streamline and upgrade the entire educational data system, parts of which had been separately managed by three different agencies. The bill proposed to create the Texas Educational Data System (TEDS), managed by one newly created board, that would allow for longitudinal analysis, be accessible to educators, policy makers, researchers, and other interested parties—and link student and teacher data. The bill even had a section providing for a study of the feasibility of using TEDS data to evaluate teachers.[36]

Although Texas is a weak-union state under the political control of Republicans, the unions and their allies were still strong enough to block. They were successful in having the offending sections on teachers voted down, and ultimately in defeating the entire bill. The following report, taken from the Texas Federation of Teachers hotline, gives a good sense of how they viewed this proposal to beef up the state's data system. For them, it was all about teachers.

> SB 1643 and related bills are all dead. The Governor's Business Council (GBC) entered this legislative session aiming to tie individual teacher appraisals and termination decision to TAKS scores [state tests] and similar measures of student achievement. TFT and educator, parent, and community allies worked with lawmakers all session long to prevent this attempt to make the overemphasis on TAKS even worse. The last gasp of this GBC initiative was a provision of HB 2238, a bill to create a new state educational data system. The GBC-inspired language in the bill called for the creation of a measure of student growth to be used in individual teachers' appraisals. However, the entire data bill died over the weekend.[37]

California is a strong-union state, and its legislature is heavily controlled by Democrats. Even so, a bill was actively considered in 2005, with the support of business leaders and the nonpartisan

Legislative Analyst's Office, that would include a unique teacher identifier in the state's data system—with language to "guarantee and ensure that no data derived from the information systems will or may be used to reward or sanction individual teachers for performance or to make employment decisions with respect to individual teachers."[38] Although this qualifier was clearly added to appease them, both the California Teachers Association (CTA) and the California Federation of Teachers (CFT) opposed the bill—and succeeded in defeating it. As the Assembly committee report noted, the CFT testified to the "hidden danger in creating a teacher identifier"—the hidden danger being that "it could easily be linked to student databases and, thus, student performance."[39]

In 2006, however, a follow-up effort was launched within the legislature, this one to modernize and expand the state's educational data capabilities by creating the California Longitudinal Teacher Integrated Data Education System (CALTIDES). This proposal, too, included a unique teacher identifier, but specifically prohibited the use of the data for evaluating, sanctioning, or paying teachers—and the unions, perhaps seeing the writing on the wall, went along with it. At least publicly. So the bill passed into law.[40] But this was hardly the end of the matter. The state's Republican governor proposed that CALTIDES receive a budget of $31 million to get it up and running—but in the state's final budget, the money didn't come through. The legislature cut most of the funding. And the next year, the same thing happened: more than $30 million was proposed, but virtually all of it was ultimately cut.[41] This is not, we should emphasize, big money: for the state spends roughly $40 billion on its public schools. The CALTIDES budget is chump change by comparison. The new program is simply a victim of the politics of blocking—which takes many forms, and is indifferent about which of the myriad veto points are relied on to do the work. This time it was the budget. Meantime, California still has no teacher identifier that can be linked to student data.

Colorado doesn't have one either. In that state, policy makers began moving toward the creation of a centralized, statewide database in 2000, when, as part of a major education reform bill, provision was made for a data reporting system managed by the state's department of education. After follow-up legislation in 2001, which provided the specifics, the state went on to construct a comprehensive database on Colorado students, which contains information on their performance, their demographics, dropout and graduation status, and more, and is capable of tracking them through time regardless of the schools they attend.[42] In 2006 a movement got underway, spearheaded by the Alliance for Quality Teaching—a bipartisan group of business, education, and political leaders—to take the next obvious step of including teacher identifiers in the data system. Although the efforts to build the student database were uncontroversial, the issue of teacher identifiers immediately led to disagreement and conflict—even within the alliance itself, which, as an inclusive organization by design, had union representation on its board.[43]

Within the legislature and in alliance-organized "stakeholder" meetings around the state, the Colorado Education Association (CEA) persistently raised the usual union objections, and did what it could to prevent a serious data reform from going through.[44] After much delay, a bill was finally passed into law in April of 2007—but it was hardly a victory for reformers.[45] Quite the contrary, it was a Rube Goldberg contraption that gave yet another creative twist to the politics of blocking. The bill did not authorize teacher identifiers. It set up a Quality Teachers Commission—with teacher representation—to study the "feasibility" of teacher identifiers over two years. If the commission decides that a system with such identifiers is feasible, it can recommend a pilot program to move it into operation—but the pilot program would have to be separately authorized by a new legislative bill. And if all this actually happens, the pilot program could not be expanded into a full-fledged reform of the data system, complete with teacher identifiers, unless the legislature passes yet another bill authorizing that step too. This is a "reform," then, that actually (and quite purposely) creates its own veto points—which give the opponents new chances to make sure that the real reform never happens. And even if it does happen, they will have delayed it by years.[46]

Texas, California, and Colorado do not have data systems with teacher identifiers because efforts to move in this direction have been blocked by the unions. But some states do have systems with teacher identifiers—and in these states, the politics of blocking has largely been overcome. Tennessee is one example. In a pioneering 1992 reform aimed at improving its public schools, Tennessee adopted the Tennessee Value Added Assessment System (TVAAS), in which students in grades two through eight were systematically tested in a range of subjects to measure their academic gains over the course of each school year—and the gains were linked to teachers and classrooms. The Tennessee Education Association (TEA) was opposed but not powerful enough to prevent the reform from going through, ultimately agreeing to accept it in return for additional school funding, guarantees that the data on individual teachers would never be made public, and that no data could be used for teacher evaluations for three years. When the three years were up, the union launched a political effort to stop the use of data for evaluation purposes—and to this day, the state itself does not use the data to evaluate teachers. It does, however, allow the districts to do so, and some do. Even in Tennessee, then, the politics of blocking has had an effect. But for the most part, the union has lost the battle. Tennessee has a well-developed state-level data system that links student and teacher data; it provides policy makers at both levels with a sophisticated informational capacity; and with performance increasingly an open book, the unions are likely to lose ground as time goes on.[47]

Florida is probably the state where union blocking has been least successful. In part, this is due to its history: its department of education began creating an automated data system, complete with student and teacher identifiers, in the 1980s—before the accountability movement picked up steam, and before the unions saw data and technology issues as salient—and by 1991 all school districts were reporting student and teacher data electronically to the state under its Florida Information Resource Network (FIRN). But the absence of blocking is also due to simple politics. When Republican Jeb Bush became governor in 1999, he used overwhelming Republican majorities in the legislature to enact a remarkably innovative program of accountability and school choice—called the A-Plus plan—and as part of this larger reform effort, the department of education (with legislative consent) built the state's Education Data Warehouse (EDW). The intention was to build on and go beyond FIRN in providing policy makers with a much more comprehensive and powerful basis for evaluating and improving the schools. The Florida Education Association (FEA) essentially played no consequential role in any of this. It fiercely objected to the A-Plus plan and did what it could to block, but was outgunned and politically marginalized. The governor and legislature got what they wanted, including—as a small part of the whole—a beefed-up data warehouse. Today, as a result, Florida has perhaps the most impressive educational data system of all the states. In the Data Quality Campaign scoring of state progress, Florida is the only state whose system qualifies on *all* of the ten dimensions.[48]

These cases do a reasonable job of illustrating the political lay of the land. There are two basic dynamics at work here. One arises because the unions regard educational data systems as threatening. However valuable good information may be to the effective operation of schools, they do not want data systems to have the capacity to generate information about the performance of teachers—and they are driven to use their power to block if they can. The second dynamic arises because information *is* valuable to state policy makers in their efforts to promote better schools, and because the rise of technology provides them with increasingly sophisticated means of *obtaining* that information and using it to good effect.

It is true that, because of the first dynamic, the unions are often able to stand in the way of better data systems. Indeed, they are doing a more potent job of it than our case studies even suggest, for there are thirty-three states (including the District of Columbia) that don't have teacher identifiers—and in many of those states, the teachers unions are powerful enough to keep the whole issue off the political agenda, so that it never even comes up for serious debate. Even so, it is hugely important that, because of the second dynamic, the unions are increasingly on the defensive—with policy makers moving, year after year, to bolster their information systems, and the unions trying to fight them off. Over the long haul, these struggles only lead in one direction. Progress—seepage—may be slow and uneven. But regression to the old days is not going to happen.

Conclusion

Efforts to bring technology to American education are subjected to a political minefield. Yes, new technologies give rise to a vast array of exciting educational possibilities that are attractive to many parents, students, and citizens. But to the powers that be, innovations of true consequence are not attractive. They are threatening—and they need to be stopped, whatever advantages they might offer to children and the nation's education system. That is why, in state after state, what we see in both the politics of virtual schooling and the politics of information is often very similar to what we see in other areas of education reform: political action by the defenders of the system—mainly the unions—to defuse change and keep the system pretty much as it is.

Even so, there is also something unique about technology that sets it apart from the other sources of education reform. It is a social force that is essentially out of control. No one is in charge of it. No one can really stop it. Its mainsprings are in the economy and society generally, not in government per se; and its innovations are being generated at such a fast pace, with such promising applications, and with such widespread appeal that—even in the public sector—there are countless openings for change. Virtual schooling is an idea whose time has come, and there are plenty of entrepreneurs eager to initiate change by taking action on their own, from the bottom up, using whatever legal avenues and loopholes they can find—and there is a demand for what they are offering, among a population increasingly tuned in to electronic modes of communicating and seeking knowledge, and among varied constituencies whose needs are clearly not being met by the traditional system. Educational data systems are also an idea whose time has come. For technology increasingly makes it possible for governments to possess comprehensive, high-quality data of direct relevance to the effective operation of schools, and it is easy for policy makers to see its enormous value.

We are witnessing the first stage of a revolution that will take many years to play out. For now, it is rather unimpressive and easy to miss. Roughly half the states have state-level virtual schools whose formal role is decidedly not to be revolutionary, but to supplement and support the regular public schools and maintain their monopoly. These virtual schools are important innovations and have great potential, but for now they are not rocking the boat. It is the cyber charters that more immediately reflect the revolution in the making, for they are the product of bottom-up entrepreneurial action and directly compete with the regular public schools: offering a full curriculum, educating the whole child, and doing it in a dramatically different way. Yet all this makes cyber charters threatening to the powers that be—and subject to political blocking in all its wondrous forms, which has been fairly successful in beating them back and keeping them in check. And then there are the ongoing efforts by states to develop their information systems. These systems are hugely important for wise, well-grounded decision making on the schools, and their capacities continue to improve year by year—but here too progress is deflated and delayed by the blocking power of the unions.

If what we are witnessing are the first halting steps toward a revolution in public education, then what comes next? How do these early developments—which barely make a dent in the traditional system, and are clearly arousing strong political opposition—go from these primitive early stirrings to a full-blown revolution? And what kind of transformation will they ultimately produce? This is what our final chapter is about.

6

A NEW ERA

This book is about two serious problems in American society—one educational, one political—and a uniquely powerful social force that carries within it the seeds of a solution to both.

The education problem is the mediocre performance of America's public schools. By any reasonable standard, the schools are not meeting the needs of twenty-first-century children—not preparing them for the workforce, not preparing them to be independent thinkers, not even ensuring that they know the basics of English, math, and science. This problem is hardly new. The nation has been aware of it for decades, and reformers have struggled to do something about it. But their push for improvement has continually been plagued by a second problem—the politics of blocking—that is more fundamental still, because it prevents the education problem from being addressed in an effective way.

The brute fact is that, in American education, policy making is not guided by what is best for children or the larger public. It is a political process driven by power. And the most powerful groups in that process are special interests, led by the teachers unions, with a stake in keeping the system as it is. Mainstream "reforms" that do little to change the system or enhance student achievement are allowed to pass through the political gates. Reforms of real consequence are vigorously resisted and watered down.

Technology holds enormous promise for schools and learning. It has the capacity to transform the "means of production" in education, allowing for individualized curricula and approaches, heightened interest and participation, more efficient allocations of resources, a much broader array of choices, and a lot more. It also has the capacity to arm the public with far better data on the schools, to put a spotlight on poor performance, and to generate information crucial to improvement. Yet precisely because technology is so consequential, it is also disruptive and threatening to the defenders of the existing system—and they are using their formidable power in the political process to try to block it. In politics, the benefits of reform don't carry the day. Power does.

So the question is, how can technology transform the schools if it faces powerful political opposition? Won't it just be limited, constrained, and co-opted by the existing system—and fail to bring about a real transformation? This chapter provides an answer. The crux of it is that, although we have focused thus far on technology's benefits for schools, and thus on its promise in helping resolve the nation's education problem, we believe that technology is also destined to help resolve the *political* problem that has prevented reformers from taking effective action. To put it simply: the seepage of technology into the system—which cannot be stopped and will continue—works slowly but inexorably to undermine the political power of the teachers unions. With their power to resist weakened over time, the floodgates will then be opened—not only for high-tech innovation, but also for a wide range of reforms that have much to contribute to American education.

The lesson of the past is that real improvement in American education cannot happen without a change in politics. Technology is going to bring that change about. Indeed, in some sense its political impact may well be its most consequential educational achievement. Yes, the benefits for schools and learning promise to be substantial. But by weakening the special interests in the political process, and by freeing policy makers to give greater weight to the interests of children and the American public, technology promises to let a thousand flowers bloom—much of it, we suspect, hybrid forms that blend the high-tech and the traditional—as the nation moves toward a school system that takes advantage of whatever works. The promise of technology, in other words, is a new era for America's schools: an era of freedom, innovation, and improvement.

The Impact of Technology on Politics

Technology is different from accountability, choice, and other education reforms. It is not really a reform at all. It is an exogenous social force that originates from outside the education system, is transforming nearly every aspect of American social life, and will keep transforming it in the decades ahead. The education system is unavoidably caught up in all this, resistance notwithstanding. It lives in a larger social environment, it depends on that environment for survival—and the environment is rapidly changing, due to the impact of an exogenous force that educators cannot control.

Exogeneity is a uniquely powerful source of change. Sixty-five million years ago, an asteroid hit the Earth—a totally exogenous event that none of the Earth's inhabitants had anything to do with, but that dramatically altered the climate of the entire planet. It created a new environment. And in this environment, new species emerged and existing ones either adapted or died out. One of the hardiest of all vertebrate animals—the dinosaurs—died out. They weren't suited to the new environment that had been thrust upon them by an exogenous event of great magnitude.[1]

We don't want to push the metaphor too far. But it is clear that technology has thrust a new environment on the education system—and there are going to be consequences. Ultimately, these consequences will be transformative. But some of them are happening even now. Of these, perhaps the most important is the technological seepage that we have discussed in prior chapters: technology is working its way into public education—by incremental means, far short of a revolution—whether the defenders of the system like it or not. They can limit it. They can fight it. But they can't completely stop it.

The sources of these early, unstoppable changes are already at work. In education's new environment, technology rapidly generates new ideas and capabilities with exciting relevance to the way children can be taught and schools organized and operated. People in the larger American society learn about these possibilities and develop new (and ever-evolving) expectations—about what they want from their education system, whether their needs are being met, and what types of schools and learning opportunities are likely to meet them. Even today, with the change process barely under way, the notion that all education should take place within the physical confines of brick-and-mortar buildings and by traditional teaching methods is clearly outmoded and old-fashioned. And this will be increasingly true as time goes on: in a thoroughly technological society, people will come to believe that they can and should have access to whatever educational opportunities that technology has to offer. The defenders of the existing system cannot stop this from happening. They cannot stop people from seeing, learning, wanting—and demanding—what their environment clearly makes possible. The implications for politics are obvious, for policy makers—although limited by the defenders' power—are nonetheless sensitive to the needs and demands of voters, and will take action when they can to try to please them.

Just as technology generates its own demand, so it also generates entrepreneurs on the supply side who envision new types of schools as vehicles for these new ideas and capabilities, and who act on whatever openings exist to establish such schools. Although the current system's defenders are powerful, the openings for entrepreneurial action are out there, and they cannot be shut off entirely. Charter laws, whether explicitly or through their gray areas, are allowing entrepreneurs to set up cyberschools that compete with the regular public schools. District officials now know that technology empowers them to attract students from other districts, and some have broken ranks with their fellow defenders, set up their own cyberschools, and taken aggressive action to increase their enrollments and revenues. State policy makers have acted as entrepreneurs on occasion too, setting up cyberschools that cover entire states and have the potential to enroll huge numbers of students. All of these entrepreneurial efforts are sure to continue in future years—and generate more schools. And all of this shapes the politics of education: creating new organizations, new constituencies, and new networks of entrepreneurs, all with a stake in new forms of education—and with the capacity, in future years, to come together on that basis, coordinate their resources, and exercise political power.

Amid these supply and demand dynamics, it is of real importance—as Christensen and his colleagues have emphasized—that district and state officials have incentives of their own to outsource some of the public schools' work to virtual schools. When kids in rural areas need AP courses or instruction in foreign languages, or when dropouts need to gain enough credits to graduate, or when gifted students need to move ahead quickly in their studies, the regular public schools may not be able to accommodate them, and the districts may not have the money to expand their services. So to public officials at both the state and district levels—who are eager to please, as long as powerful opposition doesn't get in the way—virtual schools emerge as an attractive means of providing quality services, pleasing constituents, and doing it for a reasonable cost. The most obvious result has been the rise of state-level virtual schools, which, although just supplements to what the districts are offering, have opened online learning to many thousands of American students and gotten themselves established as integral parts of the American educational landscape. As budget crunches hit and student populations grow and diversify, these virtual schools will take on more and more responsibilities over time—and more and more of the student population. And although cyber charters are being vigorously opposed in the political process, they too can be expected to grow and attract their share of students.

The seepage of technology into the public school system is natural and inexorable. It arises from the simple conjoining of new technology and the newly shaped attitudes, incentives, and opportunities of the various players in American education. In itself, this is not a revolution. Not by a long shot. But over the next decade or two, its spread and accumulation will increasingly have impacts that go well beyond the education of children, unleashing forces that relentlessly eat away at the power of the unions, weaken their ability to block, and transform the political process. And it is this transformation of the political process, not the advance of technology alone, that will open the door to the transformation of the education system—and of learning more generally.

What is this connection, then, between technology and politics? How will the seepage of technology into the system gradually undermine the power of the unions? The fact is, there are going to be several drivers of change here—all of them pushing forcefully in the same direction.

The Transcendence of Geography

Traditionally, the teaching profession in this country has been based on the geographic concentration of teachers in local schools and districts, with the districts serving as the teachers' employers. This is one of the foundations of unionization in public education. When teachers work together in the same location and share the same local employer, union organizers can personally contact all the relevant teachers quite easily, they can recruit activists to the cause, they can generate a sense of solidarity and obligation based on social connections, everyday interactions, and common occupational interests—and all of this, needless to say, hugely facilitates the process of attracting and retaining members (and their dues money). It also facilitates the kinds of coordinated actions—the willingness of members to strike, engage in work slowdowns, ring doorbells, hand out campaign literature, and the like—that the unions rely on for success in collective bargaining and politics.

Some level of geographic concentration among teachers is probably here to stay. There will always be a need for face-to-face teaching, especially for the very young, but also for adolescents—who need opportunities to work with other students in person, and to participate in athletics, the performing arts, and other activities that are inherently social. So at least some teachers will continue to gather together with students in the same physical space. But as virtual schools gain in prominence, and as larger numbers of students in the regular public schools find that *some* aspects of their education can be pursued through distance learning, more and more teaching will be carried out electronically rather than in front of student-filled classrooms—and fewer teachers will be geographically concentrated within school districts. The Florida Virtual School, for example, currently has more than 300 full-time teachers and 180 adjunct teachers, but there is no need for them to be concentrated in the same geographic place, and they are not.[2] They are dispersed throughout the state, and some even live outside it. This is just the beginning of a social dynamic that is destined to transform the geography of teaching. Concentration is giving way to dispersion, and to a corresponding diversity of employers. Increasingly, students will be taught by teachers who are located *somewhere else*, and who are *not employed* by their local school district.

When teachers are more dispersed and lack a common employer, the unions' job is far more difficult. We can already see as much by simply looking at how the unions have fared historically with private schools and (nonvirtual) charter schools. When these are the intended "bargaining units," teachers are essentially fragmented into hundreds or thousands of such units, each an employer that must be organized separately, and the unions have found it very hard to target all these separate units and mobilize teachers to join. Their track record is not good. Only about 12 percent of charter schools are unionized, and the figure is far lower (about 4–5 percent) for private schools.[3]

In important respects, technology poses even greater challenges for unions. The teachers in private and (nonvirtual) charter schools are at least geographically concentrated at the school site. But with virtual schools, even this need not be so. The teachers can be *anywhere*—they can be in another county, across the state, or in India for that matter—and there need be no geographic concentration whatever. The upshot is that, as virtual schools expand and attract students over time, the dispersion of teachers will erode the geographic concentration on which unionization is based—and this in turn will undermine the unions' power. They will have fewer members, less money, and less of what it takes to wield clout in the political process.

The geography-shattering effects of technology, we should note, are not just posing problems that are somehow unique to teachers unions. They are posing problems for unions generally—although the severity can be expected to vary, of course, depending on the nature of the work involved. As one scholar of American labor relations recently put it,

> [Traditionally, unionization in the United States] explicitly assumes that employees anticipate a continuing relationship with their employers and that union representation occurs at the workplace. The Internet defies these assumptions by creating a corps of workers with lowered physical and psychological attachments to their place of employment. . . . Admittedly, any appraisal of the future impact of information technology must be speculative. But there is already enough evidence based on the present technology to see the contours of the threat to unions. Workers whose jobs have been reshaped by the Internet (e.g., sales representatives, professionals working on a contractual basis, home workers) are not approaching unions in large numbers and unions are not successfully recruiting them. . . . All signs point to serious, perhaps unsolvable, problems for unions.[4]

The Substitution of Technology for Labor

One of the most influential and well-documented ideas in modern economics is the notion that many realms of economic activity, particularly those in the service sector—including education, the performing arts, the helping professions, and much of government—are afflicted with "Baumol's disease," a malady first identified during the 1960s by noted economist William Baumol. The idea is that these fields are extremely labor intensive by nature, cannot substitute capital for labor, and thus cannot take advantage of technologically driven gains in productivity. As a result, they suffer not only from a productivity lag relative to more progressive areas of economic activity, but also from ongoing and unavoidable cost increases. The saga of relentlessly rising costs and stagnant productivity should sound familiar to anyone who follows American public education. Since 1960, per-pupil spending on the public schools—in real (inflation-adjusted) terms—has increased by some 300 percent. Yet there has been no significant or even remotely comparable increase in student achievement.[5]

Baumol's disease, it turns out, is not a permanent affliction that will forever hobble the public schools. Information technology is the antidote. As we've seen, the new computer-based approaches to learning simply require *far fewer teachers per student*—perhaps half as many, and possibly fewer than that. Here, in fact, are some figures we collected from a few of the nation's larger, better-established cyber charters (whose names we will keep confidential): school A has 3.2 teachers per hundred students; school B has 2.4 teachers per hundred students; and school C has 1.2 teachers per hundred students. Compare these figures to those that prevail in the public schools—where the ratio is now about 6.8 teachers per hundred students, and has been rising steadily for decades—and the opportunities for real change in the educational "production function" are clear. The long-standing idea that there is something intrinsic to schooling that makes it immutably labor intensive and immune to technological change is simply not true. Maybe it was in the past. But it isn't now. Technology *can* be substituted for labor, and the dreaded consequences of Baumol's disease can be avoided: schools *can* be made more productive, and the relentless increase in costs *can* be brought under control.

These prospects augur well for education and learning, but they also have hugely important consequences for politics. With the spread of technology—and with the obvious incentives for policy makers to reduce costs by putting technology to use—the demand for teachers will be smaller than it would otherwise have been, as will the numbers of teachers participating in the education system. Although we cannot know the actual figures, the deflation of demand spells serious trouble for the unions—because it points to future limits on the pool of potential union members. In the past, as the teacher-student ratio has soared from decade to decade, the unions have been in the catbird seat: easily expanding their memberships as the pool of teachers has grown seemingly without bound. But no more. They are moving into a period of hard times, with the demand for labor dropping—and fewer teachers to grow their ranks.

The sheer size of the teachers unions is a crucial determinant of their political power. The more members they have, the more money they can wield for campaign contributions, lobbying, and advertising, the more activists they can unleash to influence election outcomes, and the more votes they can influence. The advance of technology, by bringing about new combinations of inputs that are less labor intensive, directly undermines their membership base—and as a result, tends to weaken nearly every one of the weapons that have traditionally been responsible for their power.[6]

The End of Sameness

Traditionally, teachers have taught students face-to-face in classrooms. This is the standard role, common across virtually all teachers, and has allowed for a pervasive sense of occupational sameness that has long been a very good thing for the unions. It encourages teachers to see themselves as having a common set of work interests, as being equally deserving, and as sinking or swimming together. And all of this promotes solidarity, which is critical to the unions' ability to attract members, gain their financial and emotional support, and mobilize them for economic and political ends.

It is no accident that the teachers unions are steadfast in demanding sameness, and for going to great lengths to create, nurture, and protect it—through formal rules, for example, designed to ensure that pay has nothing to do with performance, and that, if teachers simply stay on the job long enough (which anyone can do), they will have equal access to new openings and opportunities. The idea is to minimize all sources of differentiation, because they undermine the common interests and solidarity that so contribute to union success.

As we showed in Chapter Four, however, technology gives rise to a differentiation of roles among teachers. Some may still work face-to-face with students in classroom settings. But as technology seeps into the system, this will increasingly be just one of many ways that teachers take part in the learning process. Some may work with students in computer labs, handling much larger classes than today's teachers do (because the computers are taking over much of the actual teaching). Some may work with students online, but still do it in real time. Some may engage in distance learning but do it asynchronously (that is, not in real time). Some may work mainly with parents, monitoring student progress and assuring proper student oversight. Some may oversee or serve as mentors to the front-line teachers themselves. And more.

These and other jobs are very different from one another. They require different skills and backgrounds, may call for varying levels of pay (see below), offer teachers a vast array of occupational opportunities they didn't have before, encourage a level of entrepreneurialism and individualism among them as they seek out the differentiated roles they want for themselves—and in general, tend to undermine the much simpler commonality and shared interests of the traditional teaching profession. The profession of the future will be a much more differentiated and entrepreneurial one, and such a profession spells trouble for the unions. Moreover, as we noted earlier, it is destined to be a profession that will no longer concentrate teachers in common geographic locations and monopoly employers—and the resulting dispersion of teachers to new locations, combined with the diversity of employers that goes along with it, cannot help but create additional layers of differentiation that affect how teachers see their own interests.

With the rise of technology, then, the pervasive sameness that the unions have always counted on will slowly fall apart. As the years go by, they will have a harder time generating the solidarity they need to motivate teachers to join, to keep them as members, to mobilize supportive action—and to do the things successful unions need to do if they are to wield power in politics. As sameness and solidarity decline, so too will their political power.[7]

The Onslaught of Information and Transparency

Throughout most of the 1900s, the public had little objective data on which to judge the performance of the public schools. In the latter decades there were international tests of student achievement, which showed that American children didn't stack up too well relative to children in other nations. There were also NAEP and state-level tests, which reinforced concerns that the schools needed improvement. But this information was highly aggregated, giving scores for the nation as a whole or for entire states. There was precious little information for parents and citizens on how their *own* schools were performing, or how they compared to other schools.

The accountability movement began to change that by testing kids regularly, evaluating the performance of local schools, and making the information public. The advance of technology over the years, however, has boosted what is possible by many orders of magnitude—dramatically increasing the quality, detail, and sophistication of the performance information that can be collected and conveyed. It is now well within the capacity of all states to build data warehouses that store and continually update performance-based information on students, teachers, classrooms, and schools, and provide an ever-improving basis for evaluating and boosting student achievement.

Better information is destined to change politics. Above all else, it puts the spotlight on schools and districts that are performing poorly. In so doing, it sensitizes parents and citizens to the facts, gives them a well-grounded basis for making demands and taking action, and—aided by the fact that policy makers know this information too, and everyone knows they know—generates political pressure for change. It also puts the spotlight on teachers unions. This is inevitable, because unions are continually engaged in promoting the occupational interests of teachers—protecting those who are mediocre in the classroom, insisting on restrictive work rules, and all the rest—even when school performance suffers as a result. When poor performance becomes a salient public issue, the unions become subjects of scrutiny and are put on the political defensive.

The bright light of information affects their power in a direct way, because it causes them to be viewed as a source of performance problems and mobilizes other constituencies against them. It also affects their power indirectly by unleashing political pressures for them to behave more responsibly toward the schools, to stop imposing self-interested rules and requirements that undermine performance—and in general, to be more moderate in the use of their power. All of this renders them less able to pursue their interests and get their way.

A performance-based mobilization against the unions is already under way. Conservatives and Republicans, of course, have long seen the unions as the bête noire of public education. But now the unions are increasingly under attack from *within* the Democratic coalition: by high-profile leaders who speak for poor and minority children, are demanding real change—real accountability, real choice, pay for performance, more flexible dismissal policies—and are finally willing, backed by objective (and often devastating) information on the quality of urban education, to stand up within the party and challenge the unions for being obstacles to reform. Two new groups, the Democrats for Education Reform and the Education Equity Project, are playing especially prominent roles in the insurgency at this point—and they created a furor by holding a much-publicized (and massively attended) meeting at the party's 2008 presidential convention in Denver. Here is one media account, which gives a good sense of just how sharply the tables have turned:

> The evening provided a truly unusual spectacle at the convention: A megawatt group of Democrats, including Mayor Cory Booker of Newark, Mayor Adrian Fenty of Washington, D.C., and former Gov. Roy Romer of Colorado, bashed teachers' unions for an hour.... "Ten years ago when I talked about school choice, I was literally tarred and feathered," said Booker, whose celebrity at this convention, as a young African-American politician said to have the ear of Barack Obama, cannot be overstated. "I was literally brought into a broom closet by a union and told I would never win office if I kept talking about charters."...Moderator John Merrow, a reporter on The News Hour, asked Fenty what interests benefited from reactionary education policies that hurt children. The mayor took the bait. "Definitely the unions."...Summing up the panel's feelings, Roy Romer said, "In the Democratic party, you have to be realistic about some coalitions that are wedded to the past on education." He intoned, "Let's not be wedded to somebody's union rules.... An adult agenda wins too often in our present union situation."[8]

The flood of information on school performance is not the only source of political problems for the unions. Technology also enables a comprehensive linking of student data to teacher data—which in turn allows analysts to measure *teacher* performance, by determining how well each teacher is promoting the academic achievement of his or her students in the classroom. There are many ways to do this, and it is necessary, of course, that it be done fairly and accurately. But specific methodologies aside, the fact is that teacher performance *can and will be measured* as states increasingly move toward the development and use of data warehouses. And when this is done, there can no longer be any excuse for pretending that all teachers are "good" or "the same." The data will show what research (on a smaller scale) has always shown: that there are striking performance differences among teachers. Some are much better than others, and some are quite bad.[9]

This being so, and because people everywhere—parents, citizens, policy makers—are destined to know it, politics cannot help but be affected. Parents do not want their kids in the classrooms of low-performing teachers. Citizens do not want to pay the salaries of teachers who can't teach. Policy makers will have a difficult time justifying policies that make it virtually impossible to remove teachers who are *known* to be mediocre, or that pay all teachers the same even though some are demonstrably much better than others. And as these informational impacts ripple through politics, the unions will find their traditional activities—which protect the jobs of all teachers and insist that they all be paid the same—increasingly under attack.

The unions' problem, whether the information bears on the performance of schools or the performance of teachers, is ultimately the same—and intractable: once the hard data on performance exists, thanks to the advances of technology, *it will not be ignored*. It will simply be "out there," available for consumption by people who want to know the truth about their schools. In the future, low-performing schools will be found out. So will low-performing teachers. And if the unions attempt to protect them, and to continue their own activities that lead to low performance, they will pay a political price as other constituencies—more knowledgeable than ever before—insist on policies that make better sense.

More Choice, More Competition

Competition is bad for unions. This is true for unions generally and not just for the teachers unions. Broadly speaking, labor unions are best off in highly regulated, noncompetitive environments—such as the auto and steel industries before globalization, and of course virtually all forms of government. These benign settings essentially allow the unions to impose higher costs and inefficient work rules on employers with impunity, for consumers have nowhere to go and are stuck paying the price. When competition enters the picture—as it has in autos, steel, and many other American industries—this is no longer the case. Consumers can get their goods and services from organizations that produce more cost-effectively, or simply do a better job; and the unions find themselves far less powerful (and often a lot smaller). It is no accident that globalization has wrought havoc on private sector unions in the United States, and that the public sector unions—those protected from competition—are now the core of the union movement's strength. In modern American politics, the union behemoths are not the United Auto Workers, the United Steel Workers, or the Teamsters, as they were in the middle decades of the last century. The political powers are the National Education Association, the American Federation of Teachers, and other huge public sector unions like the American Federation of State, County, and Municipal Employees (AFSCME) and the Service Employees International Union (SEIU).[10]

For decades, the teachers unions have had the great advantage of living in a protected governmental environment. But technology is destined to upset the unions' good thing by generating the greatest expansion of school choice that this country's education system has ever seen—and with it, the greatest expansion of competition. The fundamentals are already in place. The burst of new educational technology offers a growing array of innovations for teaching and learning; there are countless entrepreneurs eager to take advantage of them; there is a demand for what they are offering; and despite the predictable political opposition, many new cyberschools are being created that reflect the new technology and respond to the demand. These cyberschools are schools of choice, offering students opportunities they do not have in the regular public schools. And with choice comes competition.

The competition between cyberschools and the regular public schools is educationally important. It allows kids and parents to seek out options that better suit their needs, and it gives the public schools stronger incentives to improve their performance. But it also has consequences of great importance for politics. For as cyberschools proliferate they will attract students and money away from the regular public schools, the number of teaching jobs in those schools will decline—and so will membership in the teachers unions, the resources they control, and the political power they wield. The teachers unions have always seen school choice as public enemy number one, and they have taken vigorous action—fighting vouchers, fighting charters (while publicly "supporting" them)—over the last few decades to keep it at bay. And this is precisely why: school choice undermines their power and, if truly allowed to flourish, is the ultimate survival threat. Now the threat is at their door, delivered by a force beyond their control.

As cyberschools grow and proliferate, then, the teachers unions are destined to get weaker, and the politics of education will be less in their grip. Much the same is true for their allies, the school districts. The districts are politically important because they are major employers in their localities and control lots of spending: things that elected officials at higher levels care about. But as employment and revenues drop off due to growing competition, the districts will become smaller, less consequential economically, and less powerful politically.

Competition also has the effect of boosting the political power of the school choice coalition. In the past, the choice movement drew much of its political support from market-oriented conservatives, as well as from social groups—minorities, urban parents, evangelical Christians—dissatisfied with their local public schools and eager for alternatives. Although its efforts have largely been blocked or limited by the unions, it has wielded a measure of power over the years: most states now have charter school laws, with enrollments growing steadily over time, and there are voucher and tax credit programs of various kinds around the country. But with the revolution in technology, choice has gained increasing relevance for many new constituencies—students in rural areas, AP students, homeschooling students, students needing credits to graduate, students needing flexibility in scheduling, and more—that stand to gain from the new opportunities cyberschools have to offer. And this serves to broaden the political base of the choice movement—and enhance its power.

Finally, competition not only has effects on the balance of power in the politics of education, weakening the clout of unions and districts while strengthening that of reformers, but—just as transparency does—it also creates pressure on the teachers unions to use their power in more responsible and moderate ways. When students and parents are empowered to leave schools that aren't performing, the unions know that they cannot impose whatever rigidities and costs they want on the regular public schools—and indeed, they know that if they want those schools to attract students and funds away from competitors, they need to support changes that make them more effective. Thus, to the extent that unions retain a (reduced) measure of power in future years, they are less likely to use it to hobble the public schools and prevent the adoption of productive ideas.

The Dynamics of Change

Technology is only beginning to transform the politics of education, so for now—near the end of 2008—the changes are small and difficult to notice. But that is to be expected. They are part of a larger political dynamic that, by virtue of three key properties, is capable of generating a major transformation.

The first is that these changes are mutually reinforcing. Any one change, in and of itself, may not deflate union power very much—but they all work together, in the same direction and at the same time. The rise of cyberschools leads, among other things, to the geographic dispersion of teachers, the substitution of technology for labor, the differentiation of teacher roles, and enhanced competition—all of which weaken the fundamentals of union power. Similarly, the rise of transparency puts the spotlight on poor performance, empowers the public and its policy makers to take action—and creates a hostile political environment for the unions when they try to block change and protect unproductive behavior. It is the combination of these changes, not a single silver bullet, that is ultimately so consequential for union power over the long haul.

The second key property is that, as these changes occur over time, they benefit from a positive feedback effect, and give rise to a reform process in which political success is *easier* to achieve as time goes on. Success gives way to more success, and it is essentially self-propelling once it gets going. This may seem like wishful thinking. But it is inherent in the logic of the situation. For decades the educational status quo has remained intact, despite serious concerns about school performance and despite considerable pressure for reform, because the unions and other defenders have used their massive political power to block change. The asteroid, however, has already hit. The technology revolution has set in motion one of the most profound social transformations in all human history—not an exaggeration—and the education system is inexorably caught up in it. Technology is coming to American public education, and the unions, powerful though they be, are not powerful enough to keep it out. By the nature of its operation, however, as technology becomes part of the system—through distance learning, through data warehouses and transparency—it inherently works to undermine the power of the unions. It doesn't intend to do so; it just does. And this means that, as technology advances within the education system, the unions are less and less able to block.

The corrosion of union power is the basis for the positive feedback effect. At the start of the process—as this book is being written—the unions are able to block most changes. With the rise of technology in the next five or ten years, though, union power can be expected to decline somewhat, and with it their ability to block. That being so, the door will be open a little wider to even more technological change (and other changes—see below), which in turn will corrode union power still further, reduce their blocking power still further—and open the door still wider for even more change. Thus, reform becomes easier and easier over time. It is a self-reinforcing process, driven by an internal logic that increasingly eats away at the obstacles to progress.

Which brings us to the third key property of this process of dynamic change: once the obstacles have been weakened, and once policy makers are free to make decisions that give greater weight to the requirements of effective schooling, the door is open to a broad range of reforms—not just those that involve cyberschooling. There is no doubt that computers, distance learning, and other outgrowths of technology are going to generate lots of new choices for students and parents, and shape the ways many schools are organized and operate. But the defenders have been blocking all sorts of reforms that promise to contribute to better schooling, some of them having nothing to do with new technology—and these and others like them will be able to flourish once the barriers are down.

Without union obstruction, for instance, the way is paved for more effective accountability systems. For more expansive charter systems, backed by supportive rules and financial arrangements. For additional voucher and tax credit programs that give desperately needed assistance to disadvantaged kids. For new pay systems that reward productive teachers and abandon the archaic single salary schedule. For new personnel rules that make it easier to get mediocre teachers out of the classroom. And so on.

These reforms, too, are important for more than their immediate effects on the schools. Like the cyber reforms, they also have effects on politics, and indeed they work in the same direction: by undermining the power of the teachers unions and easing the way for future reform efforts. This is true, most emphatically, of accountability and choice, the two major reform movements of our time. Accountability has the same political effects as transparency—not a coincidence, as both are rooted in accurate, objective information. Both put the spotlight on poor performance, and thus on the unions' role in poor performance, and make the unions' political lives more difficult. As accountability is strengthened, performance well measured, and schools and teachers held responsible for student learning, the unions are increasingly in trouble. The political impacts on union power are even more potent in the case of school choice. As charter schools greatly expand in number and as voucher programs for the disadvantaged are allowed to grow, more and more students will flow out of the regular public schools, employment in those schools will fall, and so will union membership, finances, and power. All this will occur simply because accountability and choice operate as they do—regardless of whether they involve computers or distance learning.

Most generally, then, technology is a force of liberation. Its obvious role is educational: it generates cyber innovations that affect the way kids can learn, teachers can teach, schools can be organized and managed, and the public and its policy makers can be informed about performance. But as these innovations seep into the education system, they unhinge its politics. And it is the political impact that is transformative: eroding the barriers that have protected the system from change, and allowing all manner of productive reforms to pass through the political gates, whether cyber or not.

The Time Horizon

It won't happen overnight. Even without any political obstacles, the early stages of technological change are difficult ones that make it hard for new schools to get a foothold and move ahead. The innovations themselves are just being developed, and haven't had a chance to improve their efficacy and really demonstrate their worth. Their value is at a low point. The costs of operation, meanwhile, are at their high point—involving all the costs of creating organizations, making initial investments, bargaining to get access, and buying equipment for students. And the new technology is out of whack with existing laws and regulations—based on geographic boundaries, "seat time" to measure attendance, the exclusion of homeschoolers, and other features of the traditional system—which will impede its development until policy makers can grope their way toward systems of rules that are better equipped to handle education in its new forms.

Absent politics, these things would work themselves out in fairly short order. The efficacy of educational technologies would grow as ideas are tested and refined over time and still more are inevitably added to the mix. The new schools would increasingly realize cost efficiencies—especially relative to the regular public schools—as their up-front investments begin to pay off, they take advantage of the low marginal costs of adding students, and the costs of technology continue to decline relative to the costs of labor. And state regulatory systems would be redesigned to use rules and funding mechanisms that make sense for the modern era of schooling, and that actively encourage and support novel forms of education.

But politics, of course, is not absent. It is the main problem, as teachers unions and other defenders use their power to defuse these processes, keep innovation at bay, and make progress much slower and more difficult than it would otherwise be. On the bright side: technology has a remarkable built-in capacity to change politics itself, largely by undermining the power of the system's defenders. When this happens, the flood gates will be open, and productive reforms of all types can flow through. But how long will this take?

Our answer is, we don't know, but it will surely take a long time. A reasonable guess is that it will take twenty years or more. There is something like a Catch-22 at work here. The defenders are at their most powerful at the very beginning, and are thus in the best possible position to block—yet technology can only undermine their power *after* it begins to make incursions into the education system: dispersing and reducing the demand for teachers, generating objective data that puts the spotlight on performance, creating lots of competition for the regular public schools, and so on. If the defenders can block from the outset, then these things and their corrosive effects won't actually happen—and the traditional system will be saved.

The Catch-22 is only apparent, however. Despite the maximal current power of the defenders, cyberschools do exist and their numbers and enrollments are growing quickly. Virtually all states, moreover, are actively involved in building data warehouses, and many are moving toward systems that link students to teachers. These are things the defenders do not want. But the information age is too pervasive and too profoundly influential a social force for them to stave off completely. Technology *is* making inroads. The defenders can block some of it, and they can weaken much of what gets through. For now. But they are fighting a losing battle. All of society is changing. And the education system—however well protected—cannot seal itself off from what is happening in the world.

As technology advances into public education, then, all the major problems are bunched into the early period of reform, and political power is stacked against it. Getting *out* of this early period is the hard part, and will probably take many years, because the politically corrosive effects of technology cannot be counted on to help very much; progress depends almost entirely on a continuation of the kind of uncontrollable seepage that has already been occurring, and that happens relatively slowly. As the years go by, however, the advance of technology will grow in significance and impact—there will be many more cyberschools (and hybrid schools) and much greater transparency about school and teacher performance—and these developments will begin to take a much bigger toll on the foundations of union power. Once this happens, blocking will be less common, change will be much easier, and it will come much faster.

In the next five or even ten years, then, change may be quite slow, and the impacts on union power imperceptible. But this is the pattern we should expect. As time goes on, the pace of change will pick up—and eventually, even if it takes decades, the transformation will come.

The Schools of the Future

As the transformation does come, or at least as the pace of change picks up and begins to take distinctive form, it is not destined to carry the American education system off into the cybersphere and leave regular schooling behind. The transformation is partly about incorporating new technologies into the way American children are educated. But it is mainly about liberating the schools from the power of special interest groups, elevating the interests of children to first priority, and generating a political process that actively embraces productive reforms of all types.

What will the schools of the future look like? No one can know the details, of course, as that is the beauty of innovation: it opens up possibilities that can't be anticipated. In general, however, there is good reason to think that certain basic properties will tend to emerge—if slowly at first—in the coming decades. The system will not be perfect. But it will be significantly different than it is now, and in our judgment significantly better. Here is what we expect, in broad outline:

Most schools will be hybrids of the traditional and the high-tech. There will be many schools in which teaching and learning occur at a distance and follow the pure cyber model—some educating the whole student as cyber charters do now, some enrolling part of the student as state-level virtual schools now do, and some doing both. Most schools, however, will be hybrids: bringing students together (at least for part of the day) for face-to-face interactions with one another and their teachers, yet also very much organized around computers, software-driven course work, Internet-based research, and distance learning for many courses that are specialized or costly for individual schools to provide on their own. The typical American child will not be attending school by sitting at home on a computer. He or she will be going to school, just as now—but the school will be very different, and many of the courses will not be taught by on-site teachers.

Schools will be more customized to students. Technology will do away with the standardized, "one size fits all" approach to education that has turned kids off and made it difficult for them to learn. In the future, students will be able to move through curricula at their own pace; have greater flexibility in choosing when and where to do their work; be better able to investigate subjects that interest them, including specialized courses that in the past would have been entirely unavailable to them; be able to conduct in-depth research using far-flung data sources; be able to "interact" with students and teachers all over the country and the world; and on and on. All of this will give students more control over their own education, make the education process much more interesting to them—and be highly motivating.

Schools will provide more effective instruction. Partly this will happen because schools will have more effective teachers. But technology itself will enhance instruction, promoting learning in ways that teachers in traditional classrooms never could. Sophisticated computer graphics, simulations, and video will communicate difficult concepts with extraordinary clarity. Software will guide students through challenging material and provide lots of opportunity for practice and feedback along the way. Formative assessments will pinpoint student weaknesses, which will then be remediated with online or teacher-led lessons crafted especially for those particular problems. The best teachers in the world—literally—will be available to any classroom at any time or place to work their magic.

Schools will be more beneficial to teachers. Teachers will have a greater variety of schools to choose from, and a greater variety of roles they might play. The typical teacher will no longer be standing in front of a classroom of twenty-five children. Indeed, there will no longer be a typical teacher: specialization and differentiation will become the norm, and the bland uniformity of the past will die a well-deserved death. With data on performance readily available, teacher pay will often depend (in part) in how much students learn, and good teachers will be rewarded for their skill and success. They will also be paid more because, as technology is substituted for labor, teachers will become more productive and less numerous, and more money can be devoted to their salaries. Mediocre teachers, meanwhile, will become much easier to identify and remove. Overall, working conditions for teachers will be more oriented by merit and achievement, more challenging and demanding, and more attractive to people with talent and ambition.

Schools will be less costly. Society can decide to spend whatever it wants on the public schools, so "costs" must be understood with that in mind. But it's all relative. Today's schools are highly labor intensive, and labor is extraordinarily costly. The schools of the future, even if most are hybrids that involve strong face-to-face components, will rely much more heavily on computers and Internet-related technologies, and will operate at a much higher capital-labor ratio than the current schools do, with fewer teachers per student (on average). Technology is relatively cheap—and it is getting cheaper all the time, as innovation and market competition drive prices down and quality up. Labor, on the other hand, is getting much more expensive. Health care benefits alone are threatening to bankrupt many school districts as things now stand. The schools of the future, then, should be far better able to provide a quality education at a cost that society can afford.

Schools will be more autonomous. The advance of technology makes it increasingly possible for new schools to rise up and survive on their own as autonomous entities, for it allows schools to attract students and hire teachers without respect to geographic boundaries and without the expense of new buildings, and it allows them to expand at relatively low marginal cost. Because of its political effects, also, there will be many more charter schools of all types, whether high-tech or not, and more voucher programs that pay for disadvantaged children to attend private schools. On the whole, then, the schools that are not autonomous—the regular public schools—will constitute a smaller portion of the population of schools receiving government funding. The schools of the future will increasingly be responsible for their own fates: living or dying on the basis of how well they do their jobs, and not sheltered or controlled by a larger bureaucracy.

Schools will be more competitive and offer more choice. Technology spells the end of monopoly in American education. The proliferation of autonomous schools, combined with their differentiation as they seek out niches and constituencies to attract enrollment, will give students and parents a much broader array of alternatives to choose from: some cyber, some hybrid, some neither, with many variations on each theme. There will be much greater variety in the universe of schools and much greater choice. And with greater choice comes greater competition—and much stronger incentives to perform: because all schools, including the regular public schools, are going to be well aware that their enrollments and revenues are not guaranteed, and that they must do their jobs well to continue attracting support.

Schools will be more accountable. Greater competition and choice lead to greater accountability on their own, because they allow students and parents to vote with their feet when school performance is inadequate—thus holding schools accountable from below. But top-down accountability will also be more effective than it currently is: in part because technology leads to the collection, analysis, and dissemination of much better information on each school's performance, and in part because the political effects of technology—which undermine union power—allow policy makers to design accountability systems that are more effective and have fewer special-interest loopholes. Accountability is therefore boosted from both ends, from the bottom up and from the top down, and the combination is likely to prove quite powerful in giving schools strong incentives to promote student learning.

Schools will do a better job of serving needy constituencies. Cyberschools provide a vehicle for incorporating the nation's million-plus homeschoolers into the education system, providing them with high-quality curricula and an organized schooling experience. Dropouts can readily take the classes they need for graduation, aided by the choice and flexibility that cybers provide them—and the graduation rate should climb. Rural kids can escape the limitations (usually due to small size and budget) of their local districts, use cybers to enroll in a full range of specialized and advanced courses, and take advantage of what the larger education system has to offer. Gifted kids, so often held back by the "least common denominator" norm in regular schools, can zoom ahead at their own speed. All of these constituencies are getting the short end of the stick under the current system. Under the new system, they will be better served—and better able to realize their potential.

Schools will do a better job of promoting social equity. Poor and minority children are the neediest of constituencies, and we deal with them separately for that reason. All too often, they are stuck in the nation's worst public schools—and the cyber revolution offers them the power to break out. Through cyberschools, they can escape their local conditions (at least in this respect) and take advantage of the same broad range of course work and educational options available to kids anywhere in the country. And as regular charter schools and voucher programs expand, they will have additional options to choose from on that dimension as well. The key is that they will have far greater choice—and they will not be trapped. Their traditional brick-and-mortar choices will be better, too. Disadvantaged kids tend to be served by the most rule-bound of the public schools systems. As the rules change to inject merit- and performance-based incentives into the public systems, schools serving poor and minority children have the most to gain.

Schools will continue to socialize students. No one is required to put their children into schools that conduct all their work at a distance and offer little or no face-to-face interaction. Parents of younger children, especially, will presumably not want that. They will tend to prefer more socially interactive settings for their kids, where children and teachers can be in the same physical place, and where values, norms, and social skills can be promoted in a directed, hands-on way. But many may feel that these social dimensions are less pressing or important—at least during school time—for older students. And in any event, even a curriculum entirely based on distance learning can involve a great deal of social interaction, sometimes much more than a traditional schooling experience would entail—it's just a different type of social interaction, one that takes place through words rather than face-to-face, but can still be extraordinarily meaningful and important to those involved. It can take place, moreover, among students who are thousands of miles apart, from different cultures, of different races and ethnicities, and may well allow for a quality of interaction that is richer and more diverse than kids often get on today's schoolyards. The notion that computers and distance learning somehow undermine the socialization of students is out of date, and based on an overly narrow notion of what socialization is. There will be plenty of social interaction going on in the schools of the future, even in pure cyber-schools. It will just take a different form than what we are used to today.

Schools will be better at doing what works. As schools become more disciplined by competition and accountability, have greater incentives to promote achievement, are more autonomous, and are freer to recruit, retain, and compensate based on merit, they will put into place those things that have been proven to succeed. Schools will improve their talent: teacher quality will rise as better teachers are attracted to the profession, low performers are weeded out, and compensation is increased. Schools will develop stronger cultures, because they will be made

up of professionals who have earned the right to be in the school
and who choose to work together for a common purpose. Curricula
will become richer and more demanding as more effective teachers and differentiated technology make rigor easier to deliver.
Schools will also be far better able to hold their own staff accountable, as technology provides ready and reliable gauges of student
progress and teachers can be held responsible for helping every
child achieve. In the world to come, schools will succeed because
they will be able—finally—to do the things that work.

Better, Not Perfect

The contrast we're drawing here is just that: a contrast. We're
pointing to changes that are likely to occur *relative* to the current
public school system, and it is by reference to this baseline that we
think the schools of the future are likely to be a big improvement.
Each of the dimensions we've discussed here is fundamental to
a quality education. Each is destined to be transformed by technology. And each should contribute to higher levels of student
achievement.

We're not saying that the schools won't have any problems.
They surely will, and along all the dimensions we've just discussed.
More competition, for example, means that more schools will fail,
and more families will experience disruptions and uncertainties as
they have to adjust. Distance learning can give rise to accountability and funding issues—and even corruption—because students
cannot be physically observed "attending" courses, doing work,
and passing tests. The incorporation of homeschoolers into cyberschools means that, because their educations were previously free
to the government, new revenues have to be found to pay for
them. The list could easily go on.

These problems, and others like them, are normal. They
are the sorts of issues that arise in any process of institutional
change, and they can readily be addressed and dealt with in reasonable ways. But still, they are problems and may subtract from

the productive functioning of the system. More generally, the social world is too complicated, organizations are too difficult to manage, and politics is too intrusive and power-driven for the schools to fly above it all and reach some sort of educational nirvana. They will always fall short in some respects. And there will always be variability in their ranks, with some doing worse than others. This too is all normal.

The great promise of technology for American education, however, is not that it makes the schools perfect or trouble free. Its great promise is that it stands to make them significantly *better* over time by transforming the underlying fundamentals of the system. It replaces the dead hand of monopoly with the dynamism of diversity and competition. It replaces the sameness of the traditional classroom model with a vast range of innovative learning alternatives. It replaces the "one size fits all" approach to students with powerful new ways of customizing schooling to the needs and interests of each individual. It replaces the uniformity of the teaching profession with differentiated roles and new career paths. It replaces job security and common pay with strong incentives tied to student learning. It replaces the weak information base of today's accountability systems with more detailed and comprehensive data. And more. Technology creates a *better* system that actively generates and nurtures *better* schools.

This emphasis on improvement, as opposed to perfection, also applies to the political side of the equation. As technology advances, it will have a profound impact on the politics of education, eroding the power of vested interests and opening the political gates for productive reforms of all types. But this shift in politics needs to be understood in relative terms. We are not saying that the new politics of education is going to function as some sort of idealized democracy in which policy makers seamlessly represent the public interest and always do the "right" thing. The new politics of education must be judged by reference to the baseline from which it departs—namely, the existing structure of education politics, in which vested interests have the power to block. What we are saying is that the new alignment of politics and power will be dramatically *better*.

Better is not ideal, and still leaves something to be desired. Yes, teachers unions and school districts will decline in power, and their interests will no longer stand in the way of change. But policy makers will still want to get reelected, and will still be responsive to groups that can affect their fates. And technology and its associated reforms can be counted on to generate new vested interests: employees, schools, companies, nonprofits, and constituencies with a stake in the new system. These groups will seek to protect their jobs, incomes, and services by organizing around those interests and exercising power on their behalf in politics—even if it is at the expense of children and quality education. Special-interest politics won't go away. It will just take a different form.

There are two important differences, however, that distinguish the new politics from the old. One is that the new supply-side actors are likely to have heterogeneous interests and functions, to be geographically dispersed, and to be part of a competitive industry—all of which militate against their coalescing into the kind of monolithic power structure that currently defends the traditional system from change. When the best interests of children call for changes in the new system, then, there will surely be political groups that want to stand in the way—but they will be weaker than the vested interests of today, and less able to block. The other difference is that the education system these new special interests will be defending is destined to be more productive and innovative than the current system, and better at promoting student achievement. So on those occasions when vested interests are able to block, they will at least be preserving a "good" status quo—possibly from changes that would make it worse.

In politics, then, as in education, there is no nirvana to look forward to. There are special interests today, and there will be special interests in the future. But the absence of some sort of perfect democracy is a given. What counts is that the new politics of education will be dramatically different from—and better than—the politics of the current system: giving less power to vested interests that for decades have prevented real reform, and creating a process that is far more supportive of progress.

A New Era

In 1983, A *Nation at Risk* warned America about the mediocrity of its public schools. When policy makers responded with energy and resolve—and untold billions of dollars—the time seemed to be ripe for change. But change of major consequence for student achievement never really came. A quarter century has gone by and, through constant frustrations and disappointments, the movement for education reform has soldiered on, making it perhaps the longest-running reform movement of any kind in American history. In some sense, this is a status to be proud of. Reformers haven't given up. Yet the brute fact is that the movement has largely been fueled by its own failure: driven to continue because its goals are never even remotely met. Performance was disappointing twenty-five years ago. It is disappointing now. And the demands of the twenty-first century are more ominous than any this nation has ever faced.

The problem is not that no one in this country knows how to construct and operate good schools. The problem is fundamentally political. All reform proposals need to make their way through the political process if they are to be authorized and put into effect, yet the political process is a minefield of power and self-interest. Any proposal of real consequence is likely to threaten the interests of powerful groups with a stake in the existing system, and to be blocked or eviscerated. The movement for education reform has failed not because the schools can't be improved. It has failed because of the politics of blocking.

This is a national problem of the first order, and until recently it had no clear solution. Power is its own protection. The teachers unions and their allies could always use their political power to defeat or resist any reforms that had the effect of taking their power away—and so it was never taken away. The political system governing public education has been in equilibrium. And the schools, therefore, have been in an equilibrium of their own, performing at consistently low levels yet protected by political power from serious structural reform. The grand equilibrium that combines the two has essentially defined the modern era of American public education: an era of great stability and continuing disappointment.

Technology is going to bring this era to an end. As befits a revolution in information—and thus in the seeking and accumulation of knowledge—it offers a dazzling array of ideas and opportunities with the capacity to transform the way children learn and the way schools are organized and operated. This is not the key to its success, however, and indeed can't be. Because what is so promising about the new educational technology—its transformative potential—is threatening to the defenders of the existing system, and they are trying to block it. The key to its success is that, as it slowly seeps into the education system, it has a range of secondary effects—through the dispersion of teachers, substitution of technology for labor, the differentiation of roles, the increase in competition, the transparency of information, and more—that inherently eat away at union and district power, and thus render their political resistance weaker and less effective as time goes on. The revolution in education is thus made possible by a revolution in politics—which erodes the politics of blocking.

These revolutions won't come suddenly. More than likely, they will take a few decades to fully flower. But what they promise is a new era for America's schools—an era in which politics and education are *both* significant improvements over the ancien régime. In the new era, the politics of education will give higher priority to the interests of children. It will be more open to innovations. And it will be more willing to do whatever works, whether the reforms involve high technology or not. The education system, meantime, will be more dynamic and productive than its

predecessor, more diverse in its offerings, and profoundly transformed by technology—but it will also keep and nurture those
aspects of the traditional system that work, and that Americans
value.

Nothing is perfect. New vested interests will surely try to
block change. And bad ideas will sometimes be adopted. But
what counts is progress. Reformers have been butting their heads
against a wall of political power for the last twenty-five years without much to show for it. Thanks to technology, that wall is coming
down—and reforms that make sense for kids and schools will be
able to flow through. This, in the end, is what the new era is all
about, and what makes it so valuable. It will allow this nation, for
the first time in recent history, to do what makes sense in trying
to improve its schools. Imagine that.

Notes

1. The Seeds of Change

1. This account is based on interviews with company executives and teachers at the school in August 2007. Shortly after the visit, Advanced Academics was acquired by DeVry Inc., one of the largest online postsecondary institutions in the world—a sign of both Advanced Academic's success and of the great potential major online companies see in K–12 online education. For more on Advanced Academics, see their Web site, http://advancedacademic.com.
2. The school is also accredited by one of the venerable regional accrediting associations, the North Central Association of Schools and Colleges.
3. The actual figure was seven hundred thousand in 2005–06, but because virtual schooling has been growing at such a fast pace it could well approach a million students today. A. G. Picciano and J. Seaman, *K–12 Online Learning: A Survey of U.S. School District Administrators* (Needham, MA: Sloan Consortium, 2007).
4. The schools are overseen by the Alliance Community Schools, a diverse board of business, government, and social service leaders from Dayton. The schools are the largest charter schools in Dayton and have been in existence since 1999. They have been managed since their inception by EdisonLearning.
5. On school performance on the 2008 Ohio Achievement Test, see Scott Elliott, "Most Charter Schools Gain; Most Dayton District Schools Saw Losses," *Dayton Daily News* (September 1, 2008).
6. National Commission on Excellence in Education, *A Nation at Risk: The Imperative for Educational Reform* (Washington, D.C.: U.S. Department of Education, April 1983).
7. For an overview of the history of American education and a summary of the challenges the nation faces, see David Tyack and Larry Cuban, *Tinkering Toward Utopia: A Century of Public School Reform* (Cambridge,

MA: Harvard University Press, 1997); Amy Gutman, *Democratic Education*, revised edition (Princeton NJ: Princeton, University Press, 1997); Diane Ravitch, *Left Back: A Century of Battles Over School Reform* (New York: Simon & Schuster, 2001); and Terry M. Moe, ed., *A Primer on America's Schools* (Stanford, CA: Hoover Press, 2001).

8. The international challenge is best summarized by Thomas Friedman, *The World Is Flat: A Brief History of the Twenty-First Century* (New York: Farrar, Straus and Giroux, 2006).

9. The evidence has been summarized in countless sources. See, for example, Paul E. Peterson, ed., *Our Schools and Our Future: Are We Still at Risk?* (Stanford, CA: Hoover Press, 2003). There is a small minority of observers who believe the nation is not at risk. The prominent statement of this position is David C. Berliner, Bruce Jessie Biddle, and Gerald R. Bracey, *The Manufactured Crisis: Myths, Fraud and the Attack on America's Public Schools* (New York: Basic Books, 1995).

10. Friedman, *The World Is Flat*.

11. In fact, computers and instructional software have been in schools for a generation without making much of a dent in education. Some observers believe that this imperviousness of the school system to technology is destined to continue into the future. See, especially, Larry Cuban, *Oversold and Underused: Computers in the Classroom* (Cambridge, MA: Harvard University Press, 2003).

2. The Need for Achievement

1. Institute of Education Sciences, National Center for Education Statistics, National Assessment of Education Progress (Washington, D.C.: U.S. Department of Education, 2007). See nces.ed.gov/naep, "Sample Questions."

2. Ibid. The actual test question reads: "What two gases make up most of the Earth's Atmosphere? A) Hydrogen and Oxygen, B) Hydrogen and Nitrogen, C) Oxygen and Carbon Dioxide, or D) Oxygen and Nitrogen." The correct answer is D, Oxygen and Nitrogen.

3. Ibid. The actual question reads: "Which is an example of water condensing? A) A puddle disappearing on a hot summer afternoon, B) Sweat forming on your forehead after you do a lot of exercise, C) Ice cubes melting when you put them out in the sun, or D) Dew forming on plants during a cold night." The correct answer is D, Dew forming on plants after a cold night.

4. NAEP is the only standardized test administered to a representative sample of elementary and secondary students nationwide, and with consistent

content and difficulty over a long period of time. The SAT and ACT are also national tests, but they are taken only by college-bound students and are not random samples even of those. State assessments are administered to every public school student in their respective states, but the tests vary widely in content and difficulty, they are subject to change from year to year, and even if somehow aggregated, they do not provide readily comparable information on student achievement nationwide.

5. NAEP is employed universally by national policy makers and education researchers to gauge how well American students are performing and progressing, and we follow that well-established practice here. We are not engaged in a detailed analysis of the NAEP data, as might be appropriate for a professional journal. We use proficiency levels—rather than scale scores or the long-term NAEP (a different set of scale scores)—because they have a straightforward conceptual meaning, and they help render the general thrust of NAEP's findings more easily understandable. Were we to use these other NAEP measures, the essence of the findings would be the same. Our goal is to simplify things and give a sense of the bigger picture. We should point out that NAEP does have its critics and that some argue, in particular, that its proficiency levels—which are more demanding than those of the states—are set at too high a level. See Tom Loveless, "Are States Honestly Reporting Test Scores?" *The Brown Center Report on American Education* (Washington, D.C.: The Brookings Institution, 2007). We cannot deal with the specifics of these arguments here. We will simply note that NAEP is widely accepted and its proficiency levels widely employed—and there are good reasons for that. NAEP is the product of a diverse panel of distinguished educators and subject matter and testing specialists, and it is overseen by the National Assessment Governing Board, another representative, expert body. Scores from NAEP are highly correlated with important educational and economic outcomes, such as high school graduation, college attendance, and lifetime earnings. Its findings of low performance are corroborated by international data (which we discuss later in the text). And when it comes to basic substance, the items that NAEP puts on these tests are all at or below grade-level for the grade of students being assessed—yet even on the items NAEP experts classify as of "medium" difficulty, about 50 percent of the nation's students typically get them wrong. Hardly an indication that they are doing well. So although proficiency can surely be measured in different ways, and the NAEP measures are not the only way to do it, we are confident that they are in the right ballpark and are at least reasonable measures of the extent to which America's students are—and are not—learning what they need to know.

6. Institute of Education Sciences, National Center for Education Statistics, National Assessment of Education Progress (Washington, D.C.: U.S. Department of Education, 2006). See nces.ed.gov/naep, "Overall Results" and "Achievement Levels," percentages of eighth-grade students proficient or advanced.

7. Ibid.

8. Institute of Education Sciences, National Center for Education Statistics, National Assessment of Education Progress (Washington, D.C.: U.S. Department of Education, 2007). See nces.ed.gov/naep, "Overall Results" and "Achievement Levels," percentages of eighth-grade students proficient or advanced.

9. Ibid. See "Overall Results" and "Achievement Levels," percentage of eighth-grade students not basic or above.

10. Ibid. See "Overall Results" and "Achievement Levels," percentages of eighth-grade students proficient or advanced.

11. Institute of Education Sciences, National Center for Education Statistics, National Assessment of Education Progress (Washington, D.C.: U.S. Department of Education, 2006). See nces.ed.gov/naep, "Sample Questions."

12. Institute of Education Sciences, National Center for Education Statistics, National Assessment of Education Progress (Washington, D.C.: U.S. Department of Education, 2005, 2006, 2007). See nces.ed.gov/naep, "Overall Results," "Results by Demographic Groups," and "Achievement Levels," percentages of fourth-, eighth-, and twelfth-grade students proficient or advanced. The percentages for the 1990s are the earliest test given in that decade; the percentages for the 2000s are the most recent test given.

13. Strictly speaking, analyses of trends over time should use the "long-term trend" data from NAEP, which includes a subset of test items and allows comparisons of equivalent tests going back to 1970. The "main NAEP," which we report on here, does report trends, but its scores are not quite as reliable measures of change as the long-term trend data. The long-term trend data, however, are limited themselves in that they include only reading and math—excluding trends on the vital subjects of science and U.S. history—and they do not report scores as "achievement levels," making it difficult to convey how well students are doing at any given time. In any case, the trends measured by both data sets show very similar patterns of progress, or the lack of it.

14. Jay P. Greene and Marcus A. Winters, "Leaving Boys Behind: Public High School Graduation Rates," *Civic Report No. 48* (New York: Manhattan Institute, April 2006).

15. Greene and Winters, "Leaving Boys Behind."

16. Ibid.

17. On the benefits of global integration, see Thomas L. Friedman, *The World Is Flat* (New York: Farrar, Straus and Giroux, 2006); especially Chapter Eight, "The Quiet Crisis."

18. On the economic causes and consequences of education domestically and internationally, see Edward P. Lazear, ed., *Education in the Twenty-first Century* (Stanford, CA: Hoover Press, 2002).

19. Organization for Economic Cooperation and Development, Programme for International Assessment, *PISA 2006: Science Competencies for Tomorrow's World*.

20. Organization for Economic Cooperation and Development, Programme for International Assessment, *Learning for Tomorrow's World: First Results from PISA 2003*.

21. Rank calculations provided by The Education Trust, Washington, D.C., 2007. See www.2.edtrust.org.

22. Institute of Education Sciences, National Center for Education Statistics, *Highlights from TIMMS 2007: Mathematics and Science Achievement in U.S. Fourth and Eighth Grade Students in an International Context* (Washington, D.C.: U.S. Department of Education, December 2008).

23. Eric A. Hanushek and Ludger Woessmann, "The Role of Cognitive Skills in Economic Development," *Journal of Economic Literature* 43(3) (Summer 2008): 607–668.

24. Eric A. Hanushek, "Some Simple Analytics of School Quality," *NBER Working Paper,* no. 10229 (January 2004).

25. Eric Hanushek, Dean T. Jamison, Eliot A. Jamison, and Ludger Woessmann, "Education and Economic Growth," *Education Next* 8(2) (Summer 2008).

26. Institute of Education Sciences, National Center for Education Statistics, *Digest of Education Statistics* (Washington, D.C.: U.S. Department of Education, 2005).

3. The Politics of Blocking

1. For more extensive treatments of the subject, see Terry M. Moe, "Union Power and the Education of Children," in Jane Hannaway and Andrew J. Rotherham, eds., *Collective Bargaining in Education* (Cambridge, MA: Harvard Education Press, 2006); and Terry M. Moe, "Teachers Unions and the Public Schools," in Terry M. Moe, ed., *A Primer on America's Schools* (Stanford, CA: Hoover Press, 2001).

2. On the early development of American public education, see David Tyack, *The One Best System* (Cambridge, MA: Harvard University Press, 1974); and Lawrence A. Cremin, *The Transformation of the School* (New York: Knopf, 1961).

3. On the rise of the teachers unions, see Marjorie Murphy, *Blackboard Unions* (Ithaca, NY: Cornell University Press, 1990); Maurice Berube, *Teacher Politics* (New York: Greenwood Press, 1988); and Myron Lieberman, *The Teacher Unions* (New York: Encounter Books, 2000).

4. For a prescient early statement about this transformation of the system, see William J. Grimshaw, *Union Rule in the Schools* (Lexington, MA: Lexington Books, 1979).

5. Current information on NEA and AFT membership statistics can be obtained from their Web sites: www.nea.org. and www.aft.org. As of late 2008, the NEA reports a membership of 3.2 million and the AFT a membership of 1.4 million.

6. Data on state-level contributions can be found on the Web at www.followthemoney.org. For contributions to federal campaigns, go to the Web site of the Center for Responsive Politics at www.opensecrets.org.

7. See, for example, Vaishali Honawar and Bess Keller, "Unions Provide Money and Personnel for Key Races," *Education Week* (November 1, 2006); and Karen Diegmueller, "Teacher Unions Try New Strategies to Lobby for Share of State Funding," *Education Week* (October 7, 1992).

8. Clive S. Thomas and Ronald J. Hrebnar, "Interest Groups in the American States," in Virginia Gray and Herbert Jacobs, eds., *Politics in the American States*, 7th ed. (Washington, D.C.: CQ Press, 1999).

9. The partisan composition of union contributions is available on the Web at both www.followthemoney.organd www.opensecrets.org.

10. For an example in which the teachers unions contributed to influential Republican legislators in Ohio, see Honawar and Keller, "Unions Provide Money and Personnel for Key Races."

11. See Charlene Haar, *The Politics of the PTA* (Edison, NJ: Transaction Publishers, 2002).

12. The exceptions are civil rights groups and representatives of the poor, which do tend to be actively involved in educational politics—although they are much less focused on education per se than the unions are. Throughout the last few decades, they have been close allies of the teachers unions, but this seems to be changing. Recently, three groups have emerged that advocate for poor and minority kids *and* are specifically focused on education reform—the Black Alliance for Educational Progress, Democrats for Education Reform, and the Education Equality Project—and they are now actively taking stands in opposition

to the teachers unions (which we briefly discuss in the concluding chapter). They are not, however, mass membership organizations with tremendous financial resources, as the unions are. See, for example, Dana Goldstein, "The Democratic Education Divide," *The American Prospect* (August 25, 2008, Web only, www.prospect.org/cs/articles?article =the_democratic_education_divide); and Gregg Toppo, "Democrats, Teachers Unions Now Divided on Many Issues," *USA Today* (September 2, 2008).

13. For an illustrative compendium of the objectives that the teachers unions actually pursue in collective bargaining, for instance, see Frederick Hess and Martin West, *A Better Bargain* (Cambridge, MA: Program on Education Policy and Governance, Harvard University, 2006).

14. For an overview of the research, see Eric A. Hanushek, "The Failure of Input-Based Schooling," *Economic Journal* 113 (2003): 64–98.

15. See, for example, Hess and West, *A Better Bargain*.

16. For a detailed overview and assessment of the early reform era, see Thomas Toch, *In the Name of Excellence* (New York: Oxford University Press, 1991). For high-profile reports, see, for example, Carnegie Forum on Education and the Economy, Task Force on Teaching as a Profession, *A Nation Prepared: Teachers for the 21st Century* (New York: Carnegie Corporation of New York, 1986); Holmes Group, *Tomorrow's Teachers* (East Lansing, MI: Michigan State University, 1986); Twentieth Century Fund, Task Force on Federal Elementary and Secondary Education Policy, *Making the Grade* (New York: Twentieth Century Fund, 1983).

17. For an informative account of various ways that the unions engaged in politics and blocked reform efforts, see Toch, *In the Name of Excellence*. For a discussion of how the unions used the reform climate to pursue their traditional objectives, see, for example, Cindy Currence, "Teachers' Unions Bringing Reform Issues to Bargaining Table," *Education Week* (May 15, 1985).

18. National Center on Education Statistics, *Digest of Education Statistics, 2008*.

19. See Eric A. Hanushek, "The Failure of Input-Based Schooling," *Economic Journal* 113 (2003): 64–98.

20. See, for example, the evidence and discussion in Caroline M. Hoxby, "What Has Changed and What Has Not," in Paul E. Peterson, ed., *Our Schools and Our Future* (Stanford, CA: Hoover Press, 2003).

21. Toch, *In the Name of Excellence*, 102.

22. On the teachers unions' political activities on these issues, see Toch, *In the Name of Excellence*, for accounts during the early reform period. For more modern developments, see, for example, Dale Ballou and Michael

Podgursky, "Gaining Control of Professional Licensing and Advancement," in Tom Loveless, ed., *Conflicting Missions?* (Washington, D.C.: The Brookings Institution, 2000); and Hess and West, *A Better Bargain*.

23. See, for example, Thomas J. Kane, Jonah E. Rockoff, and Douglas O. Staiger, "What Does Certification Tell Us about Teacher Effectiveness? Evidence from New York City," *NBER Working Paper*, no. 12155 (Cambridge, MA: National Bureau of Economic Research, 2006); for an overview, see Hanushek, "The Failure of Input-Based Schooling."

24. Perhaps the best evidence of how rarely teachers are dismissed for incompetence, and of how enormously difficult and time consuming it is for districts to do this, can be found in the research of Scott Reeder, an Illinois journalist. He has reported his findings in a series of articles, which can be found on his Web site at http://thehiddencostsoftenure.com.

25. Examples of union opposition are legion. See, for example, Joanna Richardson, "Critics Target State Teacher Tenure Laws," *Education Week* (March 1, 1995); Jennifer Medina, "Bill Would Bar Linking Class Test Scores to Tenure," *Education Week* (March 18, 2008); and Toch, *In the Name of Excellence*.

26. Michael Finnegan and Robert Salladay, "Voters Reject Schwarzenegger's Bid to Remake State Government," *Los Angeles Times* (November 9, 2005).

27. For a review of evidence, see Kate Walsh, *Teacher Certification Reconsidered: Stumbling for Quality* (Baltimore, MD: The Abell Foundation, 2001).

28. See Toch, *In the Name of Excellence*; also Kathleen Kennedy Manzo, "NC Lawmakers Revoke Teacher-Testing Plan," *Education Week* (June 17, 1998); Bess Keller, "Pennsylvania Teachers Put to Test," *Education Week* (January 9, 2002). Also, with regard to the "high quality teacher" provision of NCLB (which was a union victory on the issue of veteran teacher testing), see Julie Blair, "Unions' Positions Unheeded on ESEA," *Education Week* (November 6, 2002).

29. See Michael J. Podgursky and Matthew G. Springer, "Teacher Performance Pay: A Review," *Journal of Policy Analysis and Management* 26(4) (2007): 909–949.

30. In its 2008 resolutions, for example, the NEA states that "Any additional compensation beyond a single salary schedule must not be based on education employee evaluation, student performance, or attendance" (F-10). It also states that "performance pay schedules, such as merit pay or any other system based on an evaluation of an education employee's performance, are inappropriate" (F-9). See *NEA Handbook—2008* at www.nea.org/handbook/index.html.

31. See, for example, Ann Bradley, "D.C. Unions Assail Plan to Tie Pay to Student Achievement," *Education Week* (April 19, 1995); Alyson Klein and David J. Hoff, "Unions Assail Teacher Ideas in NCLB Draft," *Education Week* (September 19, 2007); also Toch, *In the Name of Excellence*.

32. For an overview of recent developments, see Lynn Olson, "Teacher-Pay Experiments Mounting Amid Debate," *Education Week* (October 3, 2007). Much is made of the new pay-for-performance plan adopted in Denver, in large part because it was adopted with the support of the local union. But this is an unusual departure from the national pattern, and the NEA and AFT are both opposed to pay for performance, and locals routinely fight it when the idea is proposed. The Denver plan, moreover, is not nearly as big a move as it is sometimes made out to be. It relies mainly on "performance" factors *other* than student achievement; it is voluntary for all veteran teachers (less than half of whom have yet to opt in); and it is accompanied by huge increases in funds for teacher compensation. No one will be paid less; many will be paid more. In effect, the teachers have been bought off, agreeing to very modest pay-for-performance arrangements—with little role for student test scores—in return for big increases in pay for teachers as a whole. For details on the Denver plan, see Phil Gonring, Paul Teske, and Brad Jupp, *Pay for Performance Teacher Compensation: An Inside View of Denver's ProComp Plan* (Cambridge, MA: Harvard Education Press, 2007).

33. See "Clinton Plan: 100,000 More Teachers, Smaller Class Sizes," *Education Week* (February 4, 1998); Ann Bradley, "Plan for Smaller Classes Sets Off Hiring Spree in Calif." *Education Week* (September 4, 1996); Alan Richards, "Florida Debates How to Shrink Class Sizes," *Education Week* (February 5, 2003).

34. See, for example, Hanushek, "The Failure of Input-Based Schooling"; and Eric Hanushek, "Evidence, Politics, and the Class Size Debate," in Lawrence Mishel and Richard Rothstein, eds., *The Class Size Debate* (Washington, D.C.: Economic Policy Institute, 2002).

35. In other writings, we have argued for moving from a top-down system to one that takes greater advantage of choice and competition, with schools being held accountable mainly from below. See John E. Chubb and Terry M. Moe, *Politics, Markets, and America's Schools*. There is no reason, however, that even a system that is based largely on choice and competition cannot benefit considerably from an overarching structure of rules designed to discourage unwanted behaviors, to encourage productive behaviors, and to impart the right incentives. That is essentially the strategy the nation has followed in the economic realm, where a supposedly "free market" economy is combined with a governmentally imposed

structure of rules and regulations. In the current education system, which is almost entirely top down, accountability clearly has a crucial role to play in ensuring productive performance and proper incentives. But it would continue to be desirable in a system based largely on choice and competition.

36. For a perspective on how the politics of accountability has unfolded across states, see Lance T. Izumi and Williamson M. Evers, "State Accountability Systems," in Williamson M. Evers and Herbert J. Walberg, eds., *School Accountability* (Stanford, CA: Hoover Press, 2002).

37. See, for example, the AFT report *Sizing Up State Standards, 2008*, available on its Web site at www.aft.org. It has regularly issued such reports on state academic standards since 1995.

38. John Gehring, "Mass. Teachers Blast State Tests in New TV Ads," *Education Week* (November 22, 2000).

39. See, for example, National Education Association, "Testing Plus: Real Accountability with Real Results," at www.nea.org/accountability/testplus.html; also Vaishali Honawar, "NEA Opens Campaign to Rewrite Federal Education Law," *Education Week* (July 12, 2006).

40. The unions argue that when schools and teachers perform poorly, they should be provided with additional resources, support, and training. In what it calls its "positive agenda" for NCLB reform—a good label for it, as it is an agenda entirely lacking in sanctions—the NEA says, "Schools that fail to close achievement gaps after receiving additional financial resources, technical assistance, and other supports should be subject to supportive interventions." No sanctions, no jobs put at risk, just support. It also says that when measures of student achievement are employed, they "should be used as a guide to revise instructional practices and curriculum, to provide individual assistance to students, and to provide appropriate professional development to teachers and other educators. They should not be used to penalize schools or teachers." See the NEA's publication, *ESEA: It's Time for a Change. NEA's Positive Agenda for the ESEA Reauthorization* (July 2006) at www.nea.org/esea/posagendaexecsum.html.

41. Jennifer Medina, "Bill Would Bar Linking Class Test Scores to Tenure," *New York Times* (March 18, 2008).

42. On the various actors involved, see, for example, Frederick Hess, "Reform, Resistance...Retreat? The Predictable Politics of Accountability in Virginia," in Diane Ravitch, ed., *Brookings Papers on Education Policy* (Washington, D.C.: The Brookings Institution, 2002); Paul T. Hill and Robin J. Lake, "Standards and Accountability in Washington State," in Ravitch, ed., *Brookings Papers on Education Policy*; Izumi and Evers, "State Accountability Systems"; Karla Scoon Reid, "Civil Rights Groups Split on NCLB," *Education Week* (August 31, 2005).

43. See Patrick J. McGuin, *No Child Left Behind and the Transformation of Federal Education Policy* (Lawrence: University of Kansas Press, 2006); Kevin R. Kosar, *Failing Grades: The Federal Politics of Education Standards* (Boulder, CO: Lynne Rienner, 2005); and Elizabeth H. Debray and Carl Kaestle, *Politics, Ideology, and Education* (New York: Teachers College Press, 2006).

44. See, for example, John E. Chubb, ed., *Within Our Reach: How America Can Educate Every Child* (New York: Rowman and Littlefield, 2005).

45. See, for example, Julie Blair, "Unions' Positions Unheeded on ESEA," *Education Week* (November 6, 2002); and Terry M. Moe, "A Highly Qualified Teacher in Every Classroom," in Chubb, *Within Our Reach*.

46. The details of state accountability systems can be found on the Web site of the Council of Chief State School Officers at www.ccsso.org, and the Web site of the Education Commission of the States at www.ecs.org. For overviews, see Evers and Walberg, *School Accountability*; and Chubb, ed., *Within Our Reach*.

47. This problem—that policy frameworks tend to be partly designed by actors who want them to fail—is in fact quite general and occurs across virtually all policy areas. It is not unique to education. See Terry M. Moe, "The Politics of Bureaucratic Structure," in John E. Chubb and Paul E. Peterson, eds. *Can the Government Govern?* (Washington, D.C.: The Brookings Institution, 1989).

48. Bess Keller, "NEA Files 'No Child Left Behind' Lawsuit," *Education Week* (April 20, 2005).

49. Dean Vogel, vice president of the California Teachers Association, quoted in Alyson Klein and David J. Hoff, "Unions Assail Teacher Ideas in NCLB Draft," *Education Week* (September 19, 2007).

50. On the union's attack on NCLB reauthorization generally, see, for example, Vaishali Honowar, "NEA Opens Campaign to Rewrite Federal Education Law," *Education Week* (July 12, 2006); Vaishali Honowar, "New AFT Leader Vows to Bring Down NCLB Law," *Education Week* (July 28, 2008); Klein and Hoff, "Unions Assail Teacher Ideas in NCLB Draft," *Education Week* (September 20, 2007).

51. For overviews of the choice issue, see Terry M. Moe, "Beyond the Free Market: The Structure of School Choice," *Brigham Young University Law Review*, 2008(2) 2008; and Andrew J. Coulson, *Market Education* (New Brunswick, NJ: Transaction Publishers, 1999).

52. For a discussion of the political coalitions involved in the school choice issue, see Terry M. Moe, *Schools, Vouchers, and the American Public* (Washington, D.C.: The Brookings Institution, 2001); Hubert Morken

and Jo Renee Formicola, *The Politics of School Choice* (London: Rowman and Littlefield, 1999); R. Kenneth Godwin and Frank R. Kemerer, *School Choice Tradeoffs* (Austin: University of Texas Press, 2002).

53. On the Milwaukee voucher plan, see Moe, *Schools, Vouchers, and the American Public*; and John F. Witte, *The Market Approach to Education* (Princeton, NJ: Princeton University Press, 2000).

54. See, for example, Mark Walsh, "Voucher Initiatives Defeated in Calif., Mich.," *Education Week* (November 15, 2000).

55. See, for example, Karen Diegmueller, "Despite Defeat, Choice Bill Likely to Resurface in Pa.," *Education Week* (January 8, 1992); Drew Lindsay, "Grassroots Lobbying Kills Ariz. Voucher Proposals," *Education Week* (April 26, 1995); John Gehring, "Voucher Battles Head to State Capitals," *Education Week* (July 10, 2002); and Alan Richard, "School Choice Loses Legislative Momentum," *Education Week* (June 8, 2005).

56. See, for example, Witte, *The Market Approach to Education*; Drew Lindsay, "Wisconsin, Ohio Back Vouchers for Religious Schools," *Education Week* (July 12, 1995); Jessica L. Sandham, "Florida OKs 1st Statewide Voucher Plan," (May 5, 1999); and for an overview of voucher plans across the nation, The Friedman Foundation, *The ABC's of School Choice 2007–08*, available on the foundation's Web site at www.friedmanfoundation.org.

57. Michele McNeil, "Utah Vouchers Rejected in Overwhelming Vote," *Education Week* (November 7, 2007).

58. See, for example, Marianne D. Hurst, "Colo. Supreme Court Strikes Down Voucher Law," *Education Week* (June 29, 2004); Alan Richard, "Fla. Court: Vouchers Unconstitutional," *Education Week* (January 11, 2006); Pat Kossan, "Ariz. School Voucher Programs Ruled Unconstitutional," *Arizona Republic* (May 16, 2008).

59. Zelman v. Simmons-Harris, 536 U.S. 639, 652 (2002); David Stout, "Public Money Can Pay Religious-School Tuition, Court Rules," *New York Times* (June 27, 2002).

60. This estimate is computed from The Friedman Foundation, *The ABC's of School Choice 2007–08*. The Maine and Vermont "tuitioning" programs were not included, nor were programs that simply allow parents to take a tax deduction or tax credit for educational expenses when calculating income tax. The only tax credit programs included here are those that create scholarship organizations for distributing vouchers to qualifying children.

61. Enrollment figure is from the Milwaukee Parental Choice Program, whose home page is: http://dpi.wi.gov/sms/choice.html.

62. On the history and characteristics of charter schools, see Chester E. Finn, Jr., Bruno V. Manno, and Gregg Vanourek, *Charter Schools in Action* (Princeton, NJ: Princeton University Press, 2000).

63. See, for example, David J. Hoff, "Key Democrat's Plan Would Boost Charter Schools," *Education Week* (March 19, 2008); Raymond Hernandez, "Charter Schools Gaining Support," *New York Times* (February 28, 1996).

64. For perspective on the unions' underlying opposition to charters, see Bess Keller, "Unions Turn Cold Shoulder on Charters," *Education Week* (March 27, 2002).

65. Karla Scoon Reid, "Proposal for Charter Schools Roils Detroit," *Education Week* (October 8, 2003).

66. For the unions' approach to restrictive legislation, see, for example, American Federation of Teachers, *Charter School Laws: Do They Measure Up?* (Washington, D.C.: American Federation of Teachers, 1996). On the politics of charters, see Morken and Formicola, *The Politics of School Choice*.

67. See Diana Jean Schemo, "Charter Schools Trail in Results, U.S. Data Reveal," *New York Times* (August 17, 2004); and F. Howard Nelson, Bella Rosenberg, and Nancy Van Meter, *Charter School Achievement on the 2003 National Assessment of Educational Progress*, (Washington, D.C.: American Federation of Teachers, 2004).

68. For information on TURN, see the organization's Web site at www.turnexchange.net. For more background, see Ann Bradley, "Network Seeks Union Role in Reform Efforts," *Education Week* (May 8, 1996).

69. Eric W. Robelen, "Ohio Supreme Court Narrowly Upholds State Charter Law," *Education Week* (November 1, 2006).

70. See the OEA Web site at www.ohea.org for their press release announcing their filing of the suit. Stephen Ohlemacher, "Ohio Educators File Federal Lawsuit. Teachers Union Deems Charters Illegal," *Cleveland Plain Dealer* (June 10, 2004); Catherine Candinsky, "Charter Schools Face Another Lawsuit," *Columbus Dispatch* (March 24, 2007).

71. Catherine Candinsky, "Teachers Behind Dann's Strategy?" *Columbus Dispatch* (October 2, 2007).

72. See Todd Ziebarth, "Top 10 Charter Communities by Market Share, Third Annual Edition," a report of the National Alliance of Public Charter Schools. Available on their Web site at www.publiccharters.org/2008+Market+Share. For perceptive, informative accounts of the many difficulties faced by charters, see Paul T. Hill, ed., *Charter Schools Against the Odds* (Stanford, CA: Hoover Press, 2006).

73. For an official NEA statement on the issue, see "Privatization" on its Web site at www.nea.org/privatization/index.html. For the AFT's

position, see "Privatization" on its Web site at www.aft.org/topics/privatization/index.htm.

74. This information about the number of Edison schools was provided by EdisonLearning.

75. See, for example, Mark Walsh, "Baltimore to Terminate EAI Schools Contract," *Education Week* (November 29, 1995); Mark Walsh, "Hartford Ousts EAI in Dispute over Finances," *Education Week* (January 31, 1996); Mark Walsh, "Reports Paint Opposite Pictures of Edison Achievement," *Education Week* (March 5, 2003).

4. Technology on All Fronts

1. This account is based on multiple interviews with all of the participants in the story and with a visit to Midland, Pennsylvania, and the Pennsylvania Cyber Charter School in February 2008.

2. Details on PA Cyber Charter School can be found on their Web site at www.wpccs.com.

3. A. G. Picciano and J. Seaman, *K–12 Online Learning: A Survey of U.S. School District Administrators* (Needham, MA: Sloan Consortium, 2007).

4. In 2007, Eduventures estimated the tuition revenue market size for U.S. online higher education at $6.2 billion. This estimate factors in the differences in revenue by school control and type (four-year, two-year) and accounts for both part-time and accelerated study. R. Garrett and N. Carp, *Online Higher Education Market Update 2006, Part 1: Students, Growth, and Geography* (Boston, MA: Eduventures, 2007).

5. In the Fall 2006 school term, there were 3,488,381 postsecondary students taking at least one online course nationwide. That was 19.8 percent of the country's postsecondary students. I. E. Allen and J. Seaman, *Online Nation: Five Years of Growth in Online Learning* (Needham, MA: Sloan Consortium, 2007).

6. Students can access synchronous tutoring outside of class time whether they take a course synchronously or not.

7. As a public charter school, PA Cyber is accountable to the State of Pennsylvania's Department of Education. The school must file an annual report with the department and have its finances publicly audited. Those reports and audits, from which many of the statistics in this chapter are drawn, are available from the state and posted on the school's Web site for easy public access and for full transparency—something choosing families value.

8. PA Cyber Annual Report and Pennsylvania Department of Education School Report Cards.

9. Wu Ping Lu, "Evaluation of PA Cyber's Online Program," Stanford University working paper (September 2006). Studies of online learning more broadly, covering programs still in their infancy, find student achievement gains at least as strong as those in traditional settings. See Rosina Smith, Tom Clark, and Robert L. Blomeyer, "A Synthesis of New Research on K–12 Online Learning" (North Central Regional Education Laboratory, November 2005); and Cathy Cavanaugh et al., "The Effects of Distance Learning on K–12 Student Outcomes: A Meta-Analysis" (Naperville, IL: Learning Points Associates, North Central Regional Education Lab, 2004).

10. In July 2008, after the research and writing on PA Cyber were complete, the technology firm that provides the platform for PA Cyber, Provost Systems, was purchased by EdisonLearning, a multifaceted education firm that, among other things, is one of the nation's largest managers of brick-and-mortar charter schools.

11. This account is based on interviews with all of the participants in the story and with a visit to Gurgaon, India, and Educomp in February 2008.

12. Anirudha Dutta, Prakhar Sharma, and Amar Gill, "Mr. and Mrs. India: Asia's Middle Class," *Report by CLSA Asia Pacific* (Autumn 2007); Gurcharan Das, "The Respect They Deserve: India's Rich Are Doing Well, and Good for Them—But the Growing Middle Class Is the Real Story." *Time/Asia Magazine* (November 29, 2004); and V. Phani Kumar, "India's GDP Expanded at Fastest Pace in 18 Years: Annual GDP up 9.4%, But Growth Could Moderate This Year," www.marketwatch.com (May 31, 2007).

13. Kaushik Basu, "Teacher Truancy in India: The Role of Culture, Norms and Economic Incentives" (lecture to Indian Economic Association, December 28, 2005); Michael Kremer, Nazmul Chaudhury, F. Halsey Rogers, and Karthik Muralidharan, "Teacher Absence in India: A Snapshot," *Journal of the European Economic Association* 2(2–3) 2005; Asian Human Rights Commission, "India: Primary Education: Low Coverage, Poor Quality" (online editorial, June 30, 2004, available at www.ahrchk.net); Emily Wax, "Indian Schools Try to Dismantle Barriers of Caste System," *Washington Post* (January 27, 2008).

14. For examples, see Lois Raimondo, "Homework Help from a World Away," *Washington Post* (May 14, 2006); Saritha Rai, "A Tutor Half a World Away, but as Close as a Keyboard," *New York Times* (September 7, 2005).

15. As we explain in more detail subsequently, innovations often gain footholds in new markets by not confronting the status quo directly but by offering alternatives that do not compete with any existing products or

offerings. This is a thesis for technological innovation in education offered by Harvard business professor Clayton Christensen, who has studied "disruptive innovations" in many industries. See Clayton M. Christensen, Michael B. Horn, and Curtis W. Johnson, *Disrupting Class: How Disruptive Innovation Will Change the Way the World Learns* (New York: McGraw-Hill, 2008). We discuss this book's argument in Chapter Five.

16. Tim Wiley, *Instruction for Hire: A Survey of the Private Tutoring Market*, (Boston: Eduventures, January 2007). The growth rate is expected to pick up as home Internet connectivity becomes more universal and parent comfort with international tutors develops through experience. See also Jason Overdorf, "Tutors Get Outsourced," *Business 2.0* (August 2006), 32.

17. On this non-threatening approach to market entry, again, see Christensen et al., *Disrupting Class*.

18. Toru Iiyoshi and M.S. Vijay Kumar, *Opening Up Education: The Collective Advancement of Education Through Open Technology, Open Content, and Open Knowledge* (Cambridge, MA: MIT Press, 2008).

19. Institute of Education Sciences, National Center for Education Statistics, *Digest of Education Statistics*, Table 413, (Washington, D.C.: U.S. Department of Education, 2007).

20. Ibid.

21. See Andrew Trotter, "E-Rate's Imprint Seen in Schools," *Education Week* (March 29, 2007), 12.

22. See Rhea R. Borja, "Teaching Assistants," *Education Week* (March 29, 2007), 18–22.

23. Quoted in Andrew Trotter, "Getting Up to Speed," *Education Week* (March 29, 2007), 10.

24. Anastasia Goodstein, *Totally Wired: What Teens and Tweens Are Doing Online* (New York: St. Martin's Griffin, 2007).

25. For a comprehensive analysis of the K–12 publishing industry, including basal and supplementary, see Eduventures, *K–12 Solutions Learning Markets & Opportunities, 2005* (Boston: Eduventures, February 2006).

26. Ibid., 24–35.

27. Achieve 3000 promotes itself as "the leader in differentiated instruction for K–12," and goes by the slogan, "The Power of One." Their products and services include custom portals for elementary students, "KidBiz 3000" and for secondary students, "TeenBiz 3000." See www.achieve3000.com.

28. Research on reading software is growing rapidly and is often encouraging. See, for example, "Florida Center for Reading Research Gives Lexia Reading Software Highest Ratings in Recent Published Report," *Business Wire* (June 3, 2008). The Florida center was established by Governor

Jeb Bush in January 2002, and includes some of the nation's leading authorities on reading. More on Lexia can be gleaned from their Web site, www.lexialearning.com. Soliloquy has also been successful with students, so much so that the company was recently acquired by Scientific Learning, perhaps the most research-based of all learning support firms. Founded by neuroscientists, the company introduced a program to train the brain to make fine visual distinctions more quickly and accurately, a prerequisite for reading fluency. The product, Fast ForWord, is probably the most thoroughly researched education software on the market today.

29. ALEKS is a pathbreaking software program for math instruction based on "knowledge space theory," a set of ideas developed in the 1980s and 1990s by two mathematical cognitive scientists (both seminal thinkers), professor Jean-Claude Falmagne of New York University and the University of California, Irvine, and Jean-Paul Doignon of the University of Brussels. ALEKS, which stands for Assessment and Learning in Knowledge Spaces, was developed at the University of California, Irvine, to put knowledge space theory to practical use. In essence the program provides each student a unique path through a body of mathematics by carefully assessing what students are most ready to learn, and then teaching it online, assessing mastery, and moving to the next concept or skill for which a student is best prepared. For more information, see www.aleks.com.

30. As discussed in note 27 above, see www.scilearn.com.

31. U.S. Department of Education, Institute of Education Sciences, National Center for Education Statistics, *What Works Clearinghouse*. See http://ies.ed.gov/ncee/wwc/.

32. Although so much of the promise of technology lies in the future, with rapidly accelerating innovations, the research on computer-based instruction, even in its infancy, has generally been positive. See, for example, Jeffrey Fouts, "Research on Computers and Education: Past, Present, and Future" (paper prepared for the Bill and Melinda Gates Foundation, Seattle, Washington, 2000); J. A. Kulik, "Effects of Using Instructional Technology in Elementary and Secondary Schools: What Controlled Evaluation Studies Say" (Menlo Park, CA: SRI International, 2003); and H. Waxman, Meg-Fen Lin, and Georgette M. Michko, "A Meta-Analysis of the Effectiveness of Teaching and Learning with Technology on Student Outcomes" (Naperville, IL: Learning Points Associates, North Central Regional Education Laboratory, 2003).

33. Becky Smerdon and Stephanie Cronen, *Teachers' Tools for the 21st Century: A Report on Teachers' Use of Technology*, (Washington, D.C.: National Center for Education Statistics, September 2000).

34. Estimates of teacher effects vary widely, but almost invariably show significant and substantial effects. At the upper end of effects, see William L. Sanders and S. Horn, "Research Findings from the Tennessee Value Added Assessment System (TVAAS) Database: Implications for Educational Evaluation and Research," *Journal of Personnel Evaluation in Education* 12(3) (1998): 247–256. More moderate but still substantial estimates are provided by Steve Rivkin and Eric A. Hanushek, "Teachers, Schools and Academic Achievement," *Econometrica* 73(2) (2005): 417–458. Low but significant estimates are found in B. Nye and S. Konstantopoulos, "How Large Are Teacher Effects?" *Educational Evaluation and Policy Analysis* 26 (2004): 237–258.

35. These ideas are explored in financial detail in Chris Whittle, *Crash Course* (New York: Riverhead Hardcover, 2005).

36. A complete description of this state-of-the-art lab management software can be found on the company's Web site at www.lanschool.com.

37. Public education has recently embraced an aggressive approach to preventing student academic failure and avoiding subsequent remediation and even special education. Known as "Response to Intervention" (RTI), the model calls for frequent and fine-tuned assessments of student achievement in reading and math, followed by laser-targeted interventions, designed to teach a specific skill identified as weak. RTI theory projects the classification of students into three "tiers" of need, with the neediest tier being assessed as often as every week. Across the nation, districts are attempting to implement RTI, but struggling to mesh the new model and its powerful technology with traditional roles and responsibilities. This is unfortunate, for the RTI model makes great educational sense and technologies *are* being developed to make implementation of RTI manageable. Among the most successful of these technologies is AIMSweb, a suite of assessment "probes" designed to help teachers diagnose with great accuracy student deficiencies and to manage the data necessary to track and evaluate interventions. For more on AIMSweb, see www.aimsweb.com.

38. Thomas Friedman argues that by the 1980s the flow of information internationally had already become so great that it was impossible for citizens of Eastern Bloc nations, especially those in East Germany with close historical ties with families in West Germany, not to see the vast differences in living standards between East and West. In this way, information became the unblockable force that ultimately brought down the Berlin Wall. See Friedman, *The World Is Flat,* Chapter Two, "Flattener #1: 11/9/89."

39. Atul Gawande, *Complications: A Surgeon's Notes on an Imperfect Science* (New York: Picador, 2003).

40. On the development and application of Six Sigma at General Electric, see www.1000ventures.com/business_guide/cs_quality_six-sigma_ge.html.

41. For a range of analyses of the origins and implementation of accountability, see William M. Evers and Herbert J. Walberg, eds., *School Accountability* (Stanford, CA: Hoover Press, 2002).

42. Todd V. Kern, "Trends in K–12 Enterprise Management: Are Districts Ready to Cross the Chasm?" (Boston: Eduventures, February 2007).

43. See John E. Chubb, *Within Our Reach: How America Can Educate Every Child* (Stanford, CA: Hoover Press, 2005); and Frederick M. Hess and Checker E. Finn, Jr., eds., *No Remedy Left Behind: Lessons from NCLB's First Half-Decade* (Washington, D.C.: American Enterprise Institute, 2007).

44. Eduventures, "K–12 Solutions Learning Markets & Opportunities 2005," 20–44.

45. EdisonLearning, of which John Chubb served as chief education officer until February 2008, developed and delivered one of the first formative online assessment systems in the K–12 market. This account of the challenges and opportunities presented by formative assessment is based substantially on that experience, including delivering assessments in hundreds of schools nationwide.

46. For details on the company see www.schoolnet.com.

47. Eduventures, "In Search of the Killer App." (Boston: Eduventures, April 2007).

48. State data warehouses are being driven by NCLB quite directly. NCLB's oft-criticized system for measuring student achievement by counting only student success in satisfying state proficiency standards (adequate yearly progress, or AYP) is likely to be replaced by "growth models" that give credit for student achievement *gains*, regardless of whether those gains enable a student to reach proficiency. However, these growth models, which states favor, cannot be used unless a state has a data warehouse that makes it possible to measure the progress of every student every year. To employ growth models, states now have strong incentives to develop data warehouses—which can also be used to estimate teacher effectiveness.

49. The following account was developed from the public record and from an interview with Christopher Cerf, the deputy chancellor of the New York City Public Schools, in December 2007.

50. The factors that predict and fail to predict teacher success have been the subject of more research than any other influence on student achievement. Representative studies include: Eric A. Hanushek, "Assessing the Effects of School Resources on Student Performance:

An Update," *Educational Evaluation and Policy Analysis* 19(2) (1997): 141–164; Daniel D. Goldhaber and Dominic J. Brewer, "Does Teacher Certification Matter? High School Teacher Certification Status and Student Achievement," *Educational Evaluation and Policy Analysis* 22(2) (2000): 129–145; and Linda Darling-Hammond, "Teacher Quality and Student Achievement: A Review of State Policy Evidence," *Education Policy Analysis Archives* 8(1) (2000).

51. On the state of American education twenty years after *A Nation at Risk*, see Paul E. Peterson, ed., *Our Schools and Our Future: Are We Still At Risk?* (Stanford, CA: Hoover Press, 2003).

52. John E. Chubb and Tom Loveless, eds., *Bridging the Achievement Gap* (Washington, D.C.: The Brookings Institution, 2002); Abigail M. Thernstrom and Stephan Thernstrom, *No Excuses: Closing the Racial Gap in Learning* (New York: Simon & Schuster, 2003).

53. Douglas B. Reeves, *Accountability in Action: A Blueprint for Learning Organizations* (Denver: Advanced Learning Systems, 2000). See especially, Chapter Nineteen, "The 90/90/90 Schools: A Case Study."

54. For an aggregation of the many studies on this topic, see R. Greenwald and L. V. Hedges, "The Effect of School Resources on Student Achievement," *Review of Educational Research* 66(3) (1996): 361–396.

55. E. D. Hirsch, Jr., *The Knowledge Deficit: Closing the Shocking Education Gap for American Children* (New York: Houghton Mifflin, 2007).

56. Anthony S. Bryk, Valerie E. Lee, and Peter B. Holland, *Catholic Schools and the Common Good* (Cambridge, MA: Harvard University Press, 1993).

57. David Whitman, *Sweating the Small Stuff: Inner-City Schools and the New Paternalism* (Washington, D.C.: Thomas B. Fordham Institute, 2008).

58. This is the fundamental argument that we first articulated in John E. Chubb and Terry M. Moe, *Politics, Markets, and America's Schools* (Washington, D.C.: The Brookings Institution, 1990).

5. The Resistance

1. Regarding incentive, innovation, and related problems associated with governmental supply of education, see John E. Chubb and Terry M. Moe, *Politics, Markets, and America's Schools* (Washington, D.C.: The Brookings Institution, 1990); and Andrew J. Coulson, *Market Education* (New Brunswick, NJ: Transaction Publishers, 1999). On the problems (and benefits) of governmental supply more generally, see James Q. Wilson, *Bureaucracy* (New York: Basic Books, 1989); and Clifford Winston, *Government Failure Versus Market Failure* (Washington, D.C.: AEI-Brookings, 2006).

2. Here and below, see the perspective laid out in Chubb and Moe, *Politics, Markets, and America's Schools*.

3. For an informational (and political) perspective on problems of school control and accountability, see Terry M. Moe, "Politics, Control, and the Future of School Accountability," in Paul E. Peterson and Martin West, eds., *No Child Left Behind? The Politics and Practices of School Accountability* (Washington, D.C.: The Brookings Institution).

4. As Rourke notes, "Historically, the preferred option of those seeking to have an innovative program administered imaginatively and aggressively has been to have it carried out by a new agency." See Francis E. Rourke, *Bureaucracy, Politics, and Public Policy*, 3rd ed. (Boston: Little, Brown, 1984), 179. On all the problems that make bureaucracies difficult to change and unlikely to innovate, see Wilson, *Bureaucracy*.

5. "National Teacher Survey 2005," CDW-G Teachers Talk Tech Series White Paper, available on the organization's Web site at http://newsroom .cdwg.com/features/2005 NatlTeacherSurvey.pdf.

6. Another problem, of course, is that many of today's teachers are not very tech-savvy. See, for example, Rhea R. Borja, "Teaching Assistants," *Education Week* (March 29, 2007).

7. Project Tomorrow conducts surveys of hundreds of thousands of students, as well as thousands of parents and teachers, asking them about technology and the schools. The surveys are not random samples, but they are broadly based and very informative. See their *Speak Up 2007* and *Speak Up 2006* surveys, whose findings are available on the Project's Web site at www.tomorrow.org. In addition, see "Listening to Student Voices—On Technology" (St. Paul, MN: Education|Evolving, December 2005); and Douglas Levin and Sousan Arefeh, "The Digital Disconnect: The Widening Gap Between Internet-Savvy Students and Their Schools" (Washington, D.C.: Pew Internet and American Life Project, 2002).

8. Larry Cuban, *Oversold and Underused: Computers in the Classroom* (Cambridge, MA: Harvard University Press, 2003), 178.

9. Editorial Projects in Education, "Technology Counts 2008: STEM: The Push to Improve Science, Technology, Engineering, and Mathematics," *Education Week* (March 27, 2008). Retrieved August 20, 2008, from www.edweek.org/media/ew/tc/ 2008/30state_tech_ranking.h27.pdf.

10. Editorial Projects in Education, "Technology Counts 2008."

11. Clayton M. Christensen, Curtis M. Johnson, and Michael B. Horne, *Disrupting Class: How Disruptive Innovation Will Change the Way the World Learns* (New York: McGraw-Hill, 2008).

12. For discussions of state-level virtual schools (and others), see Bill Tucker, "Laboratories for Reform: Virtual High Schools and Innovation in Public Education," *Education Sector Reports* (Washington, D.C.: Education Sector); and John Watson and Jennifer Ryan, *Keeping Pace with K–12 Online Learning* (Evergreen, CO: Evergreen Consulting Associates, November 2008). Note that our focus here is on state-level schools that provide their own courses, and thus provide students with alternatives to taking courses within their local districts. There are other types of state-initiated entities that facilitate the growth of cyber education, often by helping the districts set up their own online courses and educational activities; but because these are not alternatives to the districts, we do not discuss them here and do not include them under the heading of state-level virtual schools—even though, in the literature, some may apply that label to them. A few examples of the "schools" we are excluding: University of California College Prep, Iowa Learning Online, and MassONE (Massachusetts). Also, we don't count the widely recognized and organizationally innovative Virtual High School (Massachusetts), because it is a local rather than a state-level organization, and it enrolls students from around the entire country (with the active involvement of their local districts).

13. The data are from Editorial Projects in Education, "Technology Counts 2008." See the previous note for the criteria we used in identifying some schools as state-level virtual schools and excluding others.

14. The classic work is Jack L. Walker, "The Diffusion of Innovation Among the American States," *American Political Science Review* 63 (1969): 880–899. For a recent overview of the theoretical literature and a sophisticated empirical analysis, see Craig Volden, "States as Policy Laboratories: Emulating Success in the Children's Health Insurance Program," *American Journal of Political Science* 50 (April 2006): 294–312.

15. See, for example, Caroline Hendrie, "Florida Raises Cyber School's Fiscal Status," *Education Week* (June 11, 2003). See also "Funding Controversies Hammer Virtual Schools," *eSchool News Online* (November 1, 2003); and Tucker, "Laboratories for Reform."

16. On the legal contexts conditioning the emergence of cyber charters, see Center for Education Reform, *Charter School Laws Across the States* (2008), available on their Web site at www.edreform.com. See also Luis A. Huerta, Maria-Fernanda Gonzalez, and Chad d'Entremont, "Cyber and Home School Charter Schools: Adopting Policy to New Forms of Public Schooling," *Peabody Journal of Education* 81(1) (2006).

17. Here and throughout this section, the data on cyber charter enrollments were provided to us by the Center for Education Reform. The overall enrollment estimate of nearly one hundred thousand is an approximation. It measures "whole" student enrollments, so does not suffer from the ambiguities that attach to state-level virtual school enrollments. But the CER figures for each of the almost two hundred cyber charters are not always updated every year, so the estimate we give here is almost surely an undercount of the total cyber enrollment for 2007–08.

18. Patrick O'Donnell, "Ohio Districts Start e-Schools," *Cleveland Plain Dealer* (July 7, 2006).

19. We should note that although we do not cover Ohio in the section below, its largest cyber charters have been vigorously fought by the Ohio Federation of Teachers. See, for example, Joetta L. Sack, "Ohio Charters Targeted in Election Politics," *Education Week* (September 18, 2002); John Gartner, "Online Schools Under Scrutiny," *Wired online*, www.wired.com/techbiz/media/news/2002/05/52207(May 3, 2002); and Scott Stephens, "Online Schools Earn Mixed Grade in Ohio," *Cleveland Plain Dealer* (August 25, 2002).

20. For background and details on the Wisconsin battle over cyber charters, see the following sources, which provided the information on which the paragraphs below are based: Josh Dunn and Martha Derthick, 'The Legal Beat: Virtual Legality," *Education Next* 6(4) (2006); Sarah Carr, "Teachers Union Sues Virtual School," *Milwaukee Journal Sentinel* (September 20, 2002); Anne Davis, "Virtual Schools Grow, Learn," *Milwaukee Journal Sentinel* (November 29, 2003); Anne Davis, "Union Sues over Virtual School; WEAC Calls Funding for Non-Residents Illegal," *Milwaukee Journal Sentinel* (January 8, 2004); Amanda Paulson, "Virtual Schools, Real Concerns," *Christian Science Monitor* (May 4, 2004); Sandy Cullen, "Family a Trailblazer in Virtual Charter School," *Wisconsin State Journal* (September 25, 2005); Katherine Goodloe, "Ruling Supports Virtual Schools," *Milwaukee Journal Sentinel* (March 17, 2006); Katherine Goodloe, "Doyle Vetoes Bill on Virtual Schools," *Milwaukee Journal Sentinel* (April 19, 2006); Amy Hetzner, "Ruling Threatens Online School," *JSOnline* (www2.jsonline.com/story/index.aspx?id=693592), *Milwaukee Journal Sentinel* (December 5, 2007); Steven Walters, "Doyle Says Virtual-School Bill Must Cap Enrollment," *JSOnline* (www.jsonline.com/news/education/29542669.html), *Milwaukee Journal Sentinel* (February 25, 2008); Patrick Marley and Stacy Forster, "Doyle OKs Aid for Virtual Schools," *JSOnline* (www.jsonline.com/news/education/29527704.html), *Milwaukee Journal Sentinel* (April 7, 2008).

21. The cyber charter enrollment figure was provided to us by the Center for Education Reform. The Northern Ozaukee enrollment figure is computed (subtracting out the charter figure) from Public Policy Forum, *Southeastern Wisconsin School District Rankings, 2006–07* (Milwaukee, WI: Public Policy Forum).

22. Editorial, "Virtual School Bill a Bright Spot," *Wisconsin State Journal* (April 7, 2008).

23. The Pennsylvania struggle over cyber charters, recounted here and below, is drawn from the following sources: Kimberly Reeves, "Cyber Schools: Friend or Foe?" *The School Administrator* (October 2001); Neal McClusky, "Beyond Brick and Mortar: Cyber Charters Revolutionizing Education," Center for Education Reform, *CER Action Paper* (January 11, 2002); Shira J. Boss, "Virtual Charters: Public Schooling, at Home," *Christian Science Monitor* (January 8, 2002); Corey Murray, "Pennsylvania Seeks Fix for Troubled Cyber Schools," *eSchool News* (August 1, 2002); Eleanor Chute, "Cyber Schools Spring Up in State," *Pittsburgh Post-Gazette* (May 8, 2005); Brian Wallace, "New Cyberschool Bill," *Intelligencer Journal* (May 7, 2007); Associated Press, "Cyber School Debate Unites School Boards and Teachers Unions," *Pittsburgh Post-Gazette* (May 14, 2007); Timothy Daniels, "On Cyber School Reform, the Devil Is in the Details," *The Bulletin* (June 11, 2007).

24. This bill, HB 446, did not pass during the 2007–08 legislative session, but could obviously be resurrected and pushed during the next session.

25. Here and below, our account of the Chicago controversy draws on the following sources: Michael Coulter, "Chicago Board of Ed Approves Virtual Academy," *School Reform News* (April 2006); Diane Rado, "Charter School Going Online: State Board OKs Virtual Elementary Despite Opposition," *Chicago Tribune* (September 1, 2006); Tracy Dell'Angela, "Virtual School Opens in Face-to-Face Session: Controversial Charter Has Traditional Start," *Chicago Tribune* (September 14, 2006); Patricia Hawke, "Chicago Schools Opens Its First Virtual Elementary School," *Schools K–12* (n.d.), available at www.schoolsk-12.com/parents/htm.; Chicago Teachers Union, "Union Files Lawsuit Against Virtual Charter Proponents," CTU news release, October 4, 2006; Stephanie Banchero, "Teachers Union Sues over Cyberschool," *Chicago Tribune* (October 5, 2006); Illinois Policy Institute, "Illinois House, Teachers Union Seek to 'Pull Computers from Classroom'; Undermine Charters" (May 15, 2007), available at www.illinoispolicyinstitute.org.

26. Rado, "Charter School Going Online."

27. As of July 2008, this suit was still pending.

28. Here and below, our information on the Indiana charter dispute draws on the following: Daniel Human, "Virtual Schools Face Opposition from Teachers," *Ball State Daily News Online* (February 19, 2007); Sharlonda L. Waterhouse, "Virtual Schools May Never 'Open'," *Post-Tribune* (March 12, 2007); Gail Koch, "Virtual Charter Schools Unplugged," *Muncie Star Press* (May 3, 2007); Deanna Martin, "State Will Not Fund Virtual Schools," *Courier-Journal* (May 7, 2007); Rob Burgess, "State Drops Virtual School Funding," *Reporter-Times* (May 14, 2007); Louis Jones, "Charter Schools Lose Ball State Sponsorship," *Ball State Daily News* (May 14, 2007).

29. Julia Silverman, "Online Charter School Facing Legislative Struggles," *The World* (February 6, 2007).

30. This information on the Oregon charter dispute is drawn from: Silverman, "Online Charter School Facing Legislative Struggles"; Steven Carter, "Cyber School Charts Untested Waters," *The Oregonian* (August 24, 2005); Rob Kremer, "Update on SB1071 and Connections Academy," www.robkremer.blogspot.com (August 13, 2003); Rob Kremer, "End of Session Deal Might Kill Virtual School Before It Starts," www.robkremer.blogspot.com (August 2, 2005); Rob Kremer, "Minnis Sells Virtual Charter Schools Out to the OEA," www.robkremer.blogspot.com (August 4, 2005); (no author) "Virtual School a Victim of Its Own Success," *eSchool News* (February 15, 2007). Since the legislation was passed, two cyber charters have applied for waivers from these restrictions and been turned down by the state board. The Oregon Education Association opposed the waivers. See Julia Silverman, "State Board Says No to Online Charter School Proposals," *The World* (March 14, 2008).

31. Information on the California charter struggle draws on: K. Lloyd Billingsly, "Education Reform Threat; Battle for Control of Charter Schools Continues on Different Front," *The Daily News of Los Angeles* (June 14, 1999); Anna Bray Duff, "Charter Schools in Choke Hold," *Investor's Business Daily* (August 13, 1999); Luis A. Huerta and María-Fernanda González, "Cyber and Home School Charter Schools: How States Are Defining New Forms of Public Schooling" (New York: National Center for the Study of Privatization in Education, 2004); Cassandra Guarino, Ron Zimmer, Cathy Krop, and Derrick Chau, *Nonclassroom-Based Charter Schools in California and the Impact of SB 740* (Santa Monica, CA: Rand Corporation, 2005); Luis A. Huerta, Maria-Fernanda Gonzalez, and Chad d'Entremont, "Cyber and Home School Charter Schools: Adopting Policy to New Forms of Public Schooling," *Peabody Journal of*

Education 81(1) (2006); "History and Development of Charter School Policy in California," Legislative Analyst's Office (August 1, 2006).

32. Data on enrollments have been provided by the Center for Education Reform.

33. For an account of the bill's contents, as well as the NEA's position on its contents, see "NEA's Comments on Discussion Draft of Title I," September 14, 2007. Available at www.nea.org/esea/title1commentsdetail.html. The material on teacher identifiers is under the heading "Data Systems and Requirements."

34. Ibid.

35. See Data Quality Campaign, *2007 NCEA State P–12 Data Collection Survey Results: State of the Nation.* Available online at www .dataqualitycampaign.org/survey_results/state_of_nation.cfm.

36. Texas Legislature Online, Legislation, HB 2238 Amendments, Amendment 2. Available at www.capitol.state.tx.us/BillLookup/Amendments .aspx?LegSess=80R&Bill=HB2238.

37. TFT Legislative Hotline, "On Adjournment Date in Texas Legislature, a Report on the Fate of Some Key Bills," May 28, 2007. Available at www .unionvoice.org/tft/notice-description.tcl?newsletter_id=6499404 (as of November 2007).

38. California State Legislature, Bill Search Information, AB 1213, Amended bill as of 5/12/07, at www.legislature.ca.gov/cgi-bin/port-postquery? bill_number=ab_1213&sess=PREV&house=B&author=wyland.

39. California Assembly Committee on Education, Hearing on AB 1213, April 20, 2005, at www.leginfo.ca.gov/pub/05–06/bill/asm/ab_1201– 1250/ab_1213_cfa_20050419_101222_asm_comm.html.

40. For a discussion of the law that was finally passed (SB 1614) and the California data system, see Janet S. Hansen, "The Availability and Transparency of Education Data in California, *Education Finance and Policy 3*(1): 41–57.

41. See Ed Mendel, "Student Tracking System Receives a Failing Grade," *San Diego Union Tribune* (August 21, 2006); and Caroline An, "Student Tracking Program Trapped in Budget Limbo," *San Gabriel Valley Tribune* (July 3, 2007).

42. For an overview of the information system that the state has built on these early reforms, see "Governor's Colorado P-20 Council Brief: State Education Data Systems: How Does Colorado Measure Up?" (no author) on the Web site of the Colorado Department of Education at www.cde.state.co.us/artemis/go41/go4112d262007internet.pdf.

43. For information on the alliance, see their Web site at www. qualityteaching.org. Additional information about the alliance's

activities and tribulations was gained from interviews with someone inside the alliance, whose name we will keep confidential.

44. The alliance subsequently published a report dealing with the teacher identifier issue and highlighting the same concerns the union had raised. See Vincent Badolato, *Addressing the Need for Better Data on Teaching in Colorado: Unique Teacher Identifier: Stakeholder Process Report, 2007,* available on the Alliance's Web site at www.qualityteaching.org.

45. Colorado General Assembly, Summarized History for Bill Number SB07–140. The text of this bill is on the web at www.state.co.us/gov_dir/leg_dir/olls/sl2007a/sl_121.pdf.

46. In its "end of the first year" report (in June 2008), the commission did recommend that the state include teacher (and principal) identifiers in its data system. But the commission—which includes the president of the state teachers union—made it clear that "The teacher/principal identifier is **not** intended to sanction teachers or principals through decisions about salary, promotion, or evaluation" (emphasis in original). See Colorado Department of Education, *Quality Teachers Commission,* "Recommendations on a Teacher and Principal Identifier in Colorado," June 2008.

47. On the Tennessee system and its politics, see Jesse Fox Mayshark, "Teachers' Test Scores to Be Evaluated Before Being Released," *Knoxville News Sentinel* (May 21, 1995); Jesse Fox Mayshark, "Efforts to Weaken Education Tests Will Face Fight," *Knoxville News Sentinel* (December 1, 1996); Michael Finn, "School Testing System Called in Jeopardy," *Chattanooga Free Press* (May 11, 1997); David J. Hoff, "Delving into Data," *Education Week: Technology Counts 2006* (May 4, 2006); Nancy Zuckerbrod, "Many Teachers Dubious of Merit Pay," *Tennessee Education Association* (July 4, 2007); and Terry Bergner, Julia Stein, Jane Armstrong, and Nancy J. Smith, "Linking Teacher and Student Data: Benefits Experienced and Lessons Learned," *Data Quality Campaign* (October 2007).

48. For background and information on the Florida data system, see *Florida Department of Education Longitudinal Grant Project,* "The Florida Student and Staff Information System Chronicle," December 29, 2006. See also the material on Florida in Badolato, "Addressing the Need for Better Data on Teaching in Colorado."

6. A New Era

1. To be accurate, this is probably a slight overstatement. Though virtually all dinosaurs became extinct at some point after the asteroid's disastrous

impact, most paleontologists now believe that one type of dinosaur (ther-apods) managed to survive and evolve—into the more than ten thousand species we now refer to as birds. See Wikipedia's enlightening discussion at http://en.wikipedia.org/wiki/Dinosaur.

2. Bill Tucker, "Laboratories of Reform: Virtual High Schools and Innovation in Public Education," *EducationSector Reports* (June 2007), available at www.educationsector.org.

3. National Center for Education Statistics, *School and Staffing Survey 2003–04*. The survey and its data files (from which these figures were computed) can be accessed on the Web at http://nces.ed.gov/surveys/sass/.

4. Gary Chaison, "Information Technology: The Threat to Unions," *Journal of Labor Research* 23(2) (Spring 2002): 249–259. In our text, the first portion of the quote is taken from p. 250, the second from p. 256. On the other side of the ledger, certain unionists and scholars have expressed optimism that unions might be able to use information technology to enhance their organizing efforts—creating their own Web sites, reaching out to members and potential members, using communication to coor-dinate member behavior, and so on—but there is little evidence that these efforts, although vigorously pursued, have yielded any real gains to speak of. Membership has continued to slide. See the entire symposium in the *Journal of Labor Research*, of which the Chaison article is a part. See especially the article written by staff members of the NEA, Sam Pizzigati, Barbara Yentzer, and Ronald D. Henderson, "The School of Hard Knocks: NEA's Experience," 175–199.

5. For data on school spending, see National Center for Education Statis-tics, *Digest of Education Statistics: 2007* at http://nces.ed.gov/programs/digest/d07/. For a discussion of Baumol's logic, its application to schools, and evidence on school costs and productivity, see Eric A. Hanushek, "The Productivity Collapse in Schools," in William J. Fowler, Jr., ed., *Developments in School Finance, 1996* (Washington, D.C.: National Cen-ter for Educational Statistics, U.S. Department of Education, 1997), 183–195.

6. On the connection between union membership and political power, see, for example, Joseph B. Rose and Gary N. Chaison, "Linking Union Density and Union Effectiveness: The North American Experience," *Industrial Relations* 35(1) (January 1996): 78–105; Elimane Kane and David Marsden, "The Future of Trade Unionism in Industrialized Market Economies," *Labor and Society 13* (April 1988): 109–124; and Margaret Levi, "Organizing Power: The Prospects for an American Labor Movement," *Perspectives on Politics 1*(1) (March 2003): 45–68.

7. Two qualifications. The first is that most states have collective bargaining laws that facilitate union organizing; if a majority of teachers vote for a union, it becomes the "exclusive representative" of all teachers in the district (or charter or private school). In many districts, the contract stipulates that teachers must join the union, or else pay "agency fees" that are roughly equivalent to dues. Because of these legal advantages, the unions do not have to rely entirely or even mainly on solidarity in order to attract and retain teachers as formal members. On the other hand, the unions cannot be very successful in collective bargaining or politics if their members lack solidarity, because so much of the unions' clout depends on getting members to coordinate their behaviors—by supporting a strike, campaigning and voting for candidates, or whatever. Solidarity matters, and that is the key point here. For discussions of collective bargaining laws and public education, see, for example, Terry M. Moe, "Teachers Unions and the Public Schools," in Terry M. Moe, ed., *A Primer on America's Schools* (Stanford, CA: Hoover Press, 2001); and Myron Lieberman, *The Teacher Unions* (New York: Encounter Books, 2000).

The second qualification has to do with the basis for solidarity. The teachers unions are very much like craft unions, in the sense that they organize workers who are doing the same highly skilled jobs; it is the sameness of the members' jobs that provides the main basis for their common interests and solidarity, and this sameness is the foundation of the unions' organizational strength. It is worth noting, however, that unions can also be organized along industrial lines, and many are—such as the United Auto Workers and the United Steelworkers—with union locals typically organizing all the workers at a given plant, or within a given company. Thus, the solidarity that these industrial unions attempt to create is based on the shared interests arising from having a common employer and perhaps, in addition, from working in the same physical space—often accompanied by much emphasis on ideology. If the craft sameness of the teaching profession were broken down by technology, therefore, the teachers unions might be able to stimulate solidarity by other means. But this would be very difficult to do. In the first place, the solidarity of professional sameness is the foundation of and is woven into the warp and woof of their entire organization; and if this basis of solidarity were seriously eroded, replacing it with something different would be extremely difficult, foreign, and uncertain. It would mean a different brand of organization. In the second place, industrial unions trade heavily on workers being geographically concentrated or having common employers—and both these bases of solidarity are subject to erosion by technology. So it may well be that the lessons of industrial unionism are not going to be very helpful to teachers unions over the long run anyway. Solidarity as a determinant of union membership and success is not well studied by researchers. But for a discussion of craft and industrial unions with some attention to solidarity, see Hoyt N. Wheeler, *The Future of the American Labor Movement* (New York: Cambridge University Press, 2002).

8. Dana Goldstein, "The Democratic Divide," *The American Prospect* (August 25, 2008), Web only, retrieved October 6, 2008, from www.prospect.org/cs/articles?article=the_democratic_education_divide.

9. See, for example, William L. Sanders and Sandra P. Horn, "Research Findings from the Tennessee Value Added Assessment System (TVAAS) Database: Implications for Educational Evaluation and Research," *Journal of Personnel Evaluation in Education* 12(3) (1998): 247–256; and Eric A. Hanushek and Steven Rivkin, "Teacher Quality," in Eric A. Hanushek and Finis Welch, eds., *Handbook of the Economics of Education*, vol. 2 (Amsterdam: Elsevier, 2006).

10. On the impact of competition on U.S. labor unions, see, for example, James Peoples, "Deregulation and the Labor Market," *Journal of Economic Perspectives* 12(3) (Summer 1998): 111–130; and Henry S. Farber, "Union Membership in the United States: The Divergence Between the Public and Private Sectors," Working Paper No. 503, Princeton University, Industrial Relations Section (September 2005). On the rise of public sector unions and their roles in politics, see, for example, Andre Blais, Donald E. Blake, and Stephane Dion, *Government, Parties, and Public Sector Employees* (Pittsburgh: University of Pittsburgh Press, 1997); and Leo Troy, *The New Unionism in the New Society* (Fairfax, VA: George Mason University Press, 1994).

Index